LETTERS TO WOMEN

LETTERS TO WOMEN

EMBRACING THE
FEMININE GENIUS
IN EVERYDAY LIFE

CHLOE LANGR

TAN Books
Gastonia, North Carolina

Cover design by Caroline Green

Cover image by oxygen_8/Shutterstock

Library of Congress Control Number: 2020948816

ISBN: 978-1-5051-1515-4
Kindle ISBN: 978-1-5051-1516-1
ePUB ISBN: 978-1-5051-1517-8

Published in the United States by
TAN Books
PO Box 269
Gastonia, NC 28053
www.TANBooks.com

Printed in the United States of America

To my sweet daughter, Maeve

What an honor it is to see you grow in your own feminine genius. I love you, little bird.

Contents

Foreword

A few years ago, when Chloe Langr first asked me to be a guest on her podcast, *Letters to Women*, I was not yet familiar with her work. A podcast devoted to exploring St. John Paul II's concept of "feminine genius" was just the kind of thing I could get behind, though, and so I readily agreed.

In the course of that first conversation, I came to know Chloe as a young woman who was driven to know and share all she could about the dignity and worth of every woman. She was on fire to build up every woman in her identity as a precious daughter of God, a mission very close to my own heart.

So many women struggle to know who they are in the eyes of God. There's so much in our culture today that tells us we're not enough, that we're falling short, that we're messing up, and that we need to quash our feminine gifts and become more like men in order to find fulfillment and success in the world.

And yet, the beautiful teachings of St. John Paul II remind us that the ways in which women differ from men truly matter and that God made each woman for a special purpose. Every woman is called, in some way, to be a mother. St. John Paul II describes the world as "hungry and thirsty" for our motherhood; the world needs the gift that every mother is.

What that motherhood looks like will be different for each of us, but every woman's calling is a unique and worthy vocation.

The vast variety of ways that women hear and respond to God's call is beautifully inspiring. What Chloe has done here in this collection of essays is to lay out a tapestry of those experiences in a way that affirms our feminine gifts and strengths while fully acknowledging that it's hard sometimes and that each of us will respond to God's call in her own way.

Motherhood has the power to change the world. When women come together to encourage and affirm one another in this honored calling, we are a powerful force for the good. We, with our gifts of sensitivity, compassion, generosity, and nurturing love, have the ability to make the people God places in our lives feel uniquely known and loved. Our feminine ways of loving others are often made up of small things, hidden things the world might not often applaud or recognize.

But motherhood, with its focus on relationships and life-giving love, is no small thing. It can be everything to the soul who is blessed by the gift of a good mother. Satan knows that, and so he does all he can in the world to distract us, make us second guess ourselves, and denigrate the dignity and worth of womanhood. But thanks be to God St. John Paul II and Chloe Langr know it too.

I pray that the voices and experiences of the women highlighted here will speak to your heart about who you are in the eyes of God. I pray that you will find in them the encouragement to explore what the feminine genius means for you and the unique way God calls you to love and serve him through loving service to the people in your home, workplace, and community today. These letters are written to you, and I pray they will inspire you to find the kind of peace and joy that can only come from fully embracing the gift of your own feminine genius and becoming the woman God made you to be.

Danielle Bean

A Letter to the Woman Reading This Book

"It is thus my hope, dear sisters, that you will reflect carefully on what it means to speak of the 'genius of women', not only in order to be able to see in this phrase a specific part of God's plan which needs to be accepted and appreciated, but also in order to let this genius be more fully expressed in the life of society as a whole, as well as in the life of the Church."

—Pope St. John Paul II, *Letter to Women*

Dear sister,

What comes to mind when you think about the feminine genius? Maybe this is the first time you're exploring what those words mean. Perhaps you've heard the phrase before and wondered if it's just a buzzword that we throw around in our conversations as Catholic women. Or maybe you, like me, have spent quite a bit of time thinking about that term.

When I first heard about the feminine genius, I was in eighth grade confirmation class. I read it first in the writings of Pope St. John Paul II, a pope who recognized the beauty and dignity of women. My first impressions? I thought it was fascinating and intriguing. I wanted a part of this feminine genius, whatever it was.

But the further I got away from eighth grade and pro-gressed through high school, college, and post-graduation life as a Catholic woman, the feminine genius became some-thing less intriguing and more intimidating. The more I thought about that term, the more it seemed unattainable. In fact, I began wondering if the feminine genius was really for me.

There were parts of my story where I thought that I was too much for the feminine genius. Then, there were seasons of my life that made me think I would never be enough to claim that I was living out the feminine genius in my life. If I'm being honest with you, I was worried that I wouldn't make the cut.

I was the woman who stood in line for confession with a long list of times I'd failed to be the woman the Lord created me to be, the wife my vocation invited me to be, and the mother my parenthood offered me opportunities to become. I'd stand in line, clutching a list of ways I'd missed the mark, and ask God if he was serious about this feminine genius stuff. "Really, me, Lord? The feminine genius? Even with this list of failures and mistakes?"

I'm impatient and I have a temper. I've struggled with making time for daily prayer, and it seemed to be a miracle if I could just make it through one Rosary. There have been seasons of my life where the only prayers I could get out were prayers of anger and mistrust. I wondered if God was really a good father who shows up and keeps his promises. "Lord, I don't think you meant it to be for me, right? You can't mean that the feminine genius is for me too. I'm strug-gling to just show up in prayer; I don't think I can do the feminine genius too."

I'm addicted to perfectionism. I'm the oldest of eight, so I embody every stereotype that you have about the oldest in a big family. I love organizing things, and labelers bring joy to my life. But I also struggle with comparison. Too often, it is easy for me to compare my thoughts, words, actions, life choices, and my body to those of other women in my life, and the women on Instagram and Pinterest too. "Jesus, I think the feminine genius is for those women who have it all figured out, who truly mean it when they say they're fine. It's not for me, it's for them, right?"

In my marriage and journey to motherhood, I've carried the cross of miscarriage. Then, we couldn't get pregnant and had no answers as to why that was our experience. It seemed that everything the Lord had given me that made me a woman was broken. In the darkest parts of that season, it felt as if that brokenness was irreparable. "God, really? The feminine genius? In my daily life? You can't be serious."

So I started to dig back through the words of Pope St. John Paul II that I hadn't read since eighth grade confirmation class. If I'm being honest, I was looking for the template. The one, perfect way to live out the feminine genius—the four or five things I could put on my to-do list so that by the end of that week, I could check everything off, content that I'd done it, I'd figured out the feminine genius.

But the more I read, the more I realized that I'd been thinking of the feminine genius all wrong. I thought that an exact template was somewhere out there waiting to be discovered in the writings of Pope St. John Paul II. But instead of a list of exactly what I needed to do to embrace the feminine genius, I realized that the feminine genius isn't a cookie-cutter model for how to live authentically as a Catholic woman. It's not a box we have to stuff ourselves into. And it's for sure not something to add to our to-do list so we can cross it off.

At the end of the day, there is no one right way to live out the feminine genius. In fact, it will look different in the life of every woman because we each have our own story. As frustrating as that was for me, the longer I sat with the idea that there was a uniqueness in living the feminine genius, the more I realized the incredible freedom the Lord gives us as women.

In one of my favorite writings from his papacy, John Paul II wrote the original letter to women in 1995. In the letter, he recognized that a dialogue on the feminine genius had to start with a litany of thanks. So he began by thanking women who are mothers, wives, daughters, and sisters. He thanks women who work, women who are present in every area of life. He thanks women who are consecrated, recognizing their openness, obedience, and fidelity to the Lord. But then he pauses to thank every woman for the "simple fact of being a woman."

John Paul II recognized that every woman, regardless of her vocation, strengths, passions, crosses, and joys, brings richness into the world and helps everyone understand what it means to be an authentic and honest child of God. Not because of something she does, but because she simply is. The feminine genius, this unique way that the Lord invites us to journey back to his Sacred Heart as a woman, isn't something to do. It's something we are. Yes, we can grow and embrace the feminine genius more fully each day. Yet, at the heart of it, it's something inherent in us as women.

I wanted to discover and explore the different ways that women lived this out. How did they embrace feminine genius in their everyday, ordinary lives as Catholic women? So, three years ago, I started a podcast called *Letters to Women* because I wanted to discover an answer to that question. During each episode, I sat down across a podcast microphone with authors, doctors, artists, students, missionaries, and therapists. I had heart-to-heart conversations with women who'd discerned a call to consecrated life and women who'd discerned out of a religious order. I became friends with women who worked outside of the home and women who worked inside the home. I learned from the wisdom of women whose children played in the background and women whose hearts longed for the children they wouldn't meet this side of heaven, or the children they'd never be able to carry. I cried as women shared their stories of pain and loss. I laughed and shared in their joy and celebration.

I sat in awe of how beautifully diverse each of their stories were, but one beautiful thread ran through each of their stories. Each of those women, regardless of their vocation, passions, joys, crosses, and victories, were striving to live the life God was calling them to. At the end of every conversation, I asked each woman how she lived out the feminine genius in her daily life. I've had conversations with hundreds of women, and what I find the most beautiful about our conversations is that every single woman answers that question differently.

Within the pages of this book, I invite you to dive deep into the lives of other Catholic women and discover how they embrace their unique feminine genius in their ordinary, daily lives as women. You'll find letters from women from all walks of life. They're daughters, wives, and mothers. They're missionaries, advocates, and visionaries. But despite the wide variety of paths through life that these women walk, every single one of them is passionate about discovering the Lord's plan for their life, the way he is uniquely calling them to live out their own feminine genius. It's an honor to know and call these women friends, and I can't wait to introduce you to them and tell you more about how I've seen them live out the feminine genius in their ordinary daily lives as Catholic women. Throughout this book, you can dive into the feminine genius on your own and reflect on it with journaling questions, or read this book with other women and talk about these concepts with discussion questions.

Regardless of your journey with the feminine genius, I want to encourage you to ask yourself that question that I ask every woman on my podcast. How do you do it? How do you live out the feminine genius in your daily, ordinary life as a woman?

Your story won't look exactly like any one of the women who share their story in these chapters. Thank goodness. If it looked the same, we'd be missing out on the beauty that your story brings the world. So pull up a chair, pour yourself a cup of coffee (or two!), and let's explore and embrace the feminine genius in our ordinary, daily lives together.

In his Sacred Heart,

Chloe Langr

The Original Letter to Women - An Excerpt from the Letter of Pope St. John Paul II to Women

"I greet you all most cordially, women throughout the world!"

I would now like to speak directly to every woman, to reflect with her on the problems and the prospects of what it means to be a woman in our time. In particular I wish to consider the essential issue of the dignity and rights of women, as seen in the light of the word of God.

This "dialogue" really needs to begin with a word of thanks. As I wrote in my Apostolic Letter *Mulieris Dignitatem*, the Church "desires to give thanks to the Most Holy Trinity for the 'mystery of woman' and for every woman—for all that constitutes the eternal measure of her feminine dignity, for the 'great works of God', which throughout human history have been accomplished in and through her."

This word of thanks to the Lord for his mysterious plan regarding the vocation and mission of women in the world is at the same time a concrete and direct word of thanks to women, to every woman, for all that they represent in the life of humanity.

Thank you, women who are mothers! You have sheltered human beings within yourselves in a unique experience of joy and travail. This experience makes you become God's own smile upon the newborn child, the one who guides your child's first steps, who helps it to grow, and who is the anchor as the child makes its way along the journey of life.

Thank you, women who are wives! You irrevocably join your future to that of your husbands, in a relationship of mutual giving, at the service of love and life.

Thank you, women who are daughters and women who are sisters! Into the heart of the family, and then of all society, you bring the richness of your sensitivity, your intuitiveness, your generosity and fidelity.

Thank you, women who work! You are present and active in every area of life—social, economic, cultural, artistic and political. In this way you make an indispensable contribution to the growth of a culture which unites reason and feeling, to a model of life ever open to the sense of "mystery", to the establishment of economic and political structures ever more worthy of humanity.

Thank you, consecrated women! Following the example of the greatest of women, the Mother of Jesus Christ, the Incarnate Word, you open yourselves with obedience and fidelity to the gift of God's love. You help the Church and all mankind to experience a "spousal" relationship to God, one which magnificently expresses the fellowship which God wishes to establish with his creatures.

Thank you, every woman, for the simple fact of being a woman! Through the insight which is so much a part of your womanhood you enrich the world's understanding and help to make human relations more honest and authentic.

A Letter to the Woman Struggling to Look in the Bathroom Mirror

"What is it you want to change? Your hair, your face, your body? Why? For God is in love with all those things and he might weep when they are gone."
—St. Catherine of Siena

When God looks at you and says you are good, do you believe him? I know it's not always easy for me to see myself the way he sees me. My journey to treating myself with kindness and recognizing the goodness God sees when he gazes on me as his daughter has been a long one.

One woman who has journeyed alongside me as an incredible resource and advocate is Julia. In the time that I've been blessed to know her, she's encouraged me (and so many other women!) to remember my inherent beauty and that I'm worthy of healthy self-care practices. She's passionate about accompanying women to become more authentic and free—and that's why I'm so excited to share her letter with you.

The self-care she has introduced me to isn't just about spa days or a piece of chocolate after a hard day. That's not to say that there is something wrong with treating yourself to a relaxing weekend—and if you want to break open a bag of chocolates, I'm right there with you. But self-care extends so much further than chocolate. Beneath those desires to relax and unwind, there is a deeper cry for understanding what self-care really is and our identity as daughters of God.

If you've ever thought that you weren't worthy of the love of God, or have struggled to see yourself as good, sister, this letter is for you.

Dear sister,

When you look in the mirror, what do you see?

Is it easy to see a daughter of God who is beautiful inside and out in the face reflected in the mirror? Or is the first thing you see a woman who is tired, stressed, and overwhelmed by her life? If I had to venture a guess, I'd say you are probably experiencing the latter because, truthfully, that's how most of us feel when we look in the mirror.

Life is good and beautiful, but it can also be very hard, and that struggle shows in the face staring back at us in the mirror. Our eyes reflect the burdens we carry, the crosses we struggle with, and the scars of past hurts. The weight of these can make it difficult to see our true worth as daughters of God. The image in the mirror becomes blurred and what we see becomes distorted. Instead of seeing ourselves how God and others see us, we only see what's "wrong."

To make things worse, we use these imperfections as the barometer by which we measure our self-worth. And most of the time, that barometer tells us that we don't measure up.

Believing that you are worthy of loving yourself and being loved by God and others can be hard to embrace when all you see are mistakes and imperfections in the mirror.

I am here to tell you that you are not alone in feeling this way. You are not the only one who looks in the mirror and struggles to see the person staring back at her as someone who is lovable. In my work as a therapist, I accompanied many women through the process of letting go of the myth of perfection and embracing who they are meant to be: a daughter of God who is worthy of being loved by herself and by others.

I am here to tell you that whatever mistakes you've made in the past, whatever you are struggling with, and whatever perceived imperfections you see in yourself, they do not mean you aren't worthy of love. I am here to tell you that those perceived imperfections pale in comparison to the love that God has for you.

God's love for you is not dependent on you being perfect. And yet, that is often the impossible standard we set for ourselves. We tell ourselves that we must be the perfect woman, daughter, partner, mother, employee, or boss in order to be loved by God, by others, and by ourselves. If we make just one mistake, it can feel like we are letting everyone down, including ourselves. When we get stuck in the cycle of aiming for perfection but falling short, we fall into the trap of believing we aren't lovable because we aren't yet perfect.

Our belief that we aren't worthy of love shows up in our actions. We neglect our overall well-being because we don't believe we are worth the time and effort. And I'm not just talking about neglecting your physical appearance. I'm talking about neglecting your emotional, spiritual, relational, and physical self-care. This can show up in big ways, like when we overextend ourselves for others and leave no time for our own needs. This can also show up in little ways, like when we stay up to watch just one more episode of our favorite show (which often turns into more than just one episode) instead of going to bed on time. These decisions we make to neglect ourselves, in ways both small and large, are the ways in which we say we aren't worth the effort.

But it doesn't have to be that way. We don't have to push our well-being aside and ignore the love God has for us. We can learn to love ourselves as God loves us. This starts with self-care. Now, hear me out, sister. When you hear the term "self-care," images of pedicures, bubble baths, and other forms of pampering might come to mind, and these might seem more selfish than a path towards self-love.

However, authentic self-care goes much deeper than bubble baths and manicures. Authentic self-care is a discipline and includes any practice that has a positive and holistic impact on your physical, emotional, relational, and spiritual well-being. In other words, the practice of self-care is the practice of treating yourself as a daughter loved by God. A daughter who is loved by God (that's you!) deserves to get enough sleep, deserves to fuel her body so she has energy to tackle whatever God puts in her day, deserves to set boundaries so that she has healthy relationships, and deserves to be as free from stress and worry as she can be.

Practicing self-care isn't always easy. In fact, it can sometimes feel more like a discipline than selfish pampering. For example, getting enough sleep is far less fun than staying up late. Saying no to a request to volunteer to take on an additional work project can be tough to do in the moment even though saying no to it allows you to say yes to something else that is a priority for you. Making time for silence and prayer can be a challenge with a busy day ahead. But all of these are ways in which you can honor your needs (which are just as important as other people's).

Whether you are a new mother, a seasoned mom, a wife, or a single woman, it's dangerously easy to prioritize other people's needs at the expense of your own. In the moment, putting someone else's needs above yours may seem like the selfless thing to do. But if you aren't making time for your own needs in addition to serving others, it can backfire on you. Instead of feeling rejuvenated and fulfilled, you may start to feel drained, overwhelmed, stressed, and resentful. Recognizing your worth and practicing self-care can help restore balance in your life.

Sister, don't be afraid to say to yourself, "I am worthy of love," because it is true. You don't need to prove your worth to anyone. It has already been proven by the simple (yet profound) fact that you are created and loved by God. Don't be afraid to embrace this truth. Welcome it with open arms and be transformed by God's love for you.

We are all on this journey together, and I am walking it right along with you.

Julia

Julia Marie Hogan, LCPC, is a counselor in Chicago and owner of Vita Optimum Counseling & Consulting, LLC. She also leads workshops and writes on topics related to self-care, relationships, and mental health. Her book, It's Ok to Start with You, *is all about the power of embracing your authentic self through self-care, and she is currently working on her second book which will be published in 2021. She is passionate about empowering individuals to be their most authentic selves. You can find more information about her work at juliamariehogan.com.*

Questions for Reflection

1. What is a way that you can start practicing holistic self-care in your daily life?
2. What is one, tangible thing you can do today to embrace the fact that you are worthy of love?
3. What unique gifts and talents has God given to you? Is he inviting you to say no to some opportunities in order to be able to say yes to opportunities where your gifts and talents can truly come alive?

Questions for Conversation

1. Recall a time that you have felt the love of God the Father in your life.
2. What specific area of your life do you struggle with self-care? Why is that area a place where it is hard to see yourself as worthy of love?
3. How can you strive to honor your dignity as a daughter of God?

Come Holy Spirit, living in Mary. Help me reject the lies that I am not enough for the Lord, or that I have to prove my worth in order to earn his love. Steady in my heart that I am a daughter of God, who created me and calls me beloved. Amen.

A Letter to the Woman Reconsidering Her Relationship with Her Body

"The body, and it alone, is capable of making visible what is invisible: the spiritual and the divine. It was created to transfer into the visible reality of the world the mystery hidden since time immemorial in God [God's love for man], and thus be a sign of it."

—Pope St. John Paul II

Pope St. John Paul II writes that our bodies reveal the reality of God. But if you're turning to this letter, maybe you—like me—have doubted that. By the age of thirteen, over half of girls growing up in the United States are unhappy with their bodies.[1] By the time we're seventeen years old, 78 percent of us share that feeling.

---

[1] "Get the Facts," National Organization for Women, accessed October 21, 2020, https://now.org/now-foundation/love-your-body/love-your-body-whats-it-all-about/get-the-facts/#:~:text=One%20study%20reports%20that%20at,the%20time%20girls%20reach%20seventeen.&text=When%20asked%20%E2%80%9CAre%20you%20happy,their%2060s%20answered%20%E2%80%9Cyes%E2%80%9D.

Mary is a dear friend who has walked this journey of exploring and embracing the feminine genius with me since I was in high school. I've admired her bravery as she strives for healing in her own life, and I consider it a great honor to call her my friend.

In our friendship together, Mary has taught me so much about reassessing the way I speak about, treat, nourish, and move my body as a woman striving for sainthood, and I know that I'm not the only one who has been encouraged by Mary to live out the feminine genius in my daily life as a Catholic woman. She recognizes and honors the feminine genius in the lives of women around her.

If you're longing for encouragement as you reconsider your relationship with your body, sister, this letter is for you.

Dear Sister,

If you're about to flip the page and skip this chapter, expecting another body positive poem or self-love letter encouraging you to embrace every roll, smile at the sight of cellulite, or delight in the absence of a thigh gap, this letter is for you. After reading countless articles from well-intended authors on incredible healing journeys, I've not experienced those emotions towards my body by the time I'm done reading. To genuinely find joy in the very characteristics of my earthly home that have brought me to tears, stirred up painful conversations, caused me to avoid mirrors, made meal times stressful and clothes shopping a nightmare sounded pointless and impossible.

"Is it possible that the issue wasn't your willpower but that your body was asking for carbs because it needed them?" my dietitian asked. I was stunned—that possibility had never crossed my mind. Her question was in response to my frustration with discipline on low-carb diets in years past. The potential that my need to try harder wasn't the issue but that my body was telling me what it needed and that I could trust those signals was jarring. If my appetite wasn't something that needed suppression but attention and proper nourishment, I needed to rethink many food rules I'd lived by for years.

My desire to be well informed and appropriately nourish my body led to years of research on food plans and exercise regimens. I found myself bewildered over what I thought about food and the many approaches—organic, keto, gluten free, paleo—to the point that I felt more lost than when I had started. Every diet preached conflicting information about what qualified as good or bad food, correct timing of meals, and ideal portion sizes.

This letter is for the woman who has read excellent body positive posts only to get partially through and realize the underlying theme is gratitude for your body because it grew another human, yet you've never been pregnant. And you may feel guilt for not "having a reason" to be carrying around more weight than your ideal body would. This letter is for you if you've been hopping on and off diets during your teenage years and adulthood, finding some "success" here and there only to deduce that your willpower is the problem. This letter is for you if you've sucked in your stomach while pictures were taken, internalized a hurtful comment about your body, or kept a drawer of clothes that will fit when you lose the weight you want to.

What if our initial goal wasn't *loving* our bodies but seeking more neutral ground? What if, instead, we chose to become curious about our relationship with food rather than condemning our eating habits? Is it worth considering the ways we actually enjoy moving our bodies rather than engaging in the latest workout that promises an unmatched ability to burn fat? What if the conversation became less about which diet allowed for which food groups and more about which textures, spices, and flavor combinations made up your favorite meals?

This letter is for you.

It's a baffling experience to live in a culture where the standards and characteristics of a "perfect body" change every decade of our lives. You have likely seen the tabloids in a grocery store checkout line advertising diets that will have you fitting in your high school jeans in no time. Let's pause and ponder that for just a second. Our bodies are meant to change shape throughout our lives, and I'm not just referring to pregnancy. There's a reason that our body looks different at age seven than age sixteen. And twenty-seven, and forty-five, and so on.

Think back to when you were seven or eight. You were probably in the midst of losing and growing new teeth, learning fractions, and riding bikes with the neighbor kids. Back then, you probably didn't avoid pasta like the plague, experience your confidence crumbling while looking in the mirror, skip the ice cream because you promised yourself that you were going to be "really good today," or reminisce on your skinny days when seeing old pictures. What happened between then and now? If you're like me, you started tuning in to the ways female figures in your life talked about and responded to the changes in their own bodies. Did you overhear aunts and cousins discussing the efficacy of black colored clothing to give the illusion of a slimmer build? Did you watch your mom's beautiful friends, who couldn't be more talented or lovely in your eyes, dismiss compliments? During holiday meals, did you repeatedly hear "My diet starts tomorrow" or "Thankfully, I'm wearing my stretchy pants today"?

And if you're like me, you ventured into the preteen years by starting a diet with moms, sisters, and cousins, promising to keep one another accountable while dreaming of a new, smaller sized wardrobe in the near future. Suddenly, eating meals turned into logging points, appetites became something to be suppressed, and exercise was a form of punishment. Instead of normalizing the biological processes happening in our bodies as they changed shape, we fought back with weekly weigh-ins, cutting more foods from the acceptable list, and frequenting MyFitnessPal to log those macros. A few weeks passed, and after falling off and on the diet wagon, I found myself defeated, weighing the same (or even more) and battling a roaring appetite. As usual, biology won and I was crushed.

Are these scenarios familiar? It's painful to recount the number of times I have experienced this self-defeating cycle in my own life. But what if it were the diets that failed me and not I that failed them? What would it be like to eat with friends and fill your plate with the types and amounts

of foods that you were interested in and not according to
what you saw the skinniest folks choosing? Is it possible that
the way the clothing item was created is the problem and
not your body's shape? What if turning away from diets that
have failed you could be a step towards deeper intuition with
what your body is telling you?

You have the power to experience this freedom. Seriously! Every person has the ability to transform the way they
approach food and speak to and about their body. Movement and food will be a part of our lives until the day we
die. What kind of relationship do you want with them? The
turning point in my journey came while I was leading a
small group of college-aged women. I was horrified at the
thought of these captivating twenty-year-old ladies speaking
to their bodies the way I did to mine. But wasn't it normal
for a woman to be perpetually unhappy with her figure? I
believe that this is common, but not normal. After watching
a dear friend thank her body for how it carried her through a
workout, fuel herself in cooperation with her hunger signals,
and demonstrate detachment from a certain size by donating
clothes that didn't fit, I was very curious. Up to this point,
I'd only heard women vocalize shame and frustration about
their stubborn waistlines and lack of discipline around food.
I wanted something different: a relationship with food and
movement marked by freedom and confidence.

Working with my dietitian involved lots of exploration.
We took a deep dive into which foods I considered good and
bad, what textures and flavors created a pleasant eating experience, and what my relationship with exercise had been like.
She inquired about cultural expectations, family approaches,

and opinions I'd formed about my body. In the months that followed, I walked away from exercises I despised: running, burpees, and walking lunges. When I experimented with different kinds of training, I learned that swimming, Pilates, and biking were empowering workouts that left me rejuvenated and grateful for my body's strength. As specific foods became less of a fixated, guilty eating experience, I felt free to consume them when I wanted while also reaching for other foods.

Slowly, food began returning to its proper role of nourishing me instead of controlling me. Clothing shifted to a protective garment against the elements and not a number that dictated my worth. Finally, the brain space dominated by food stress and confusion started to dissipate as my body and I began to work together. This can absolutely happen for you too. Recreating a mindset that's been deeply impacted by diet culture is counter-cultural. Hard work and time are required to transform your wellness beliefs and behaviors.

My hope is that this reconsideration process doesn't stop with you. There are many women surrounding you attuned to your journey: daughters, neighbors, coworkers, and cousins.

This letter is for them too.

Mary

Mary Khadivi is a Kansas City native, the second of five children, and a KSU graduate with her B.S. in Animal Science. Some of her fondest college memories include taking a lambing class, serving on the hospital ministry team, and meeting her dearest friends. In her spare time, you can find her attempting to learn Farsi, swing dancing, watching makeup tutorials, and starting a new book without finishing the last one. Her ideal day includes a holy hour, car rides in the country, snuggling her pets, and being barefoot. You can connect with her on Instagram @merrymary93 or via email at khadivimary@gmail.com.

Questions for Reflection

1. How have you been impacted by today's diet culture? Are there things that you'd like to reconsider when it comes to the way that you feed and move your body?
2. What are some ways you communicate to your body and about your body? How do you speak about your reflection in the mirror and the food you consume?
3. When is the last time you thanked God for your body?

Questions for Conversation

1. What are some ways that today's culture, your family of origin, and the opinions of others have informed your understanding of your body?
2. Our bodies are meant to change throughout our lives. Was there a season in your life when you became more critical about the way your body looks or how it moves? What caused that change in the way you spoke about your body?
3. How would reconsidering your relationship with your body impact the conversations that you have with friends, family, coworkers, and even strangers?

Come Holy Spirit, living in Mary. Stir up in me a curiosity about how I speak about and interact with food and movement in my daily life. When I'm tempted to condemn myself or to give into despair or frustration, speak your truth into my heart. Give me the courage to reconsider my relationship with my body, the body that you created. Amen.

A Letter to the Woman Searching for the Truth about Her Body

"The 'revelation of the body' helps us in some way discover the extraordinary nature of what is ordinary."

—Pope St. John Paul II

When women were asked about whether they'd want to know more about their fertility, 60 percent of women said they'd like to learn more or expressed a desire to learn.[2] Learning more about your fertility and charting your cycle is a big decision, but what you learned in health class back in high school probably didn't give you enough information. To make it tougher on us, all of the options we have as women to be more aware of our fertility aren't guaranteed to be mentioned in our yearly visit to the OB-GYN.

It wasn't until I was in college that I truly grew in appreciation of what John Paul II had to say about the reality of our bodies as men and women and how the way we are made reflects the reality of who God is. Part of my growth in the appreciation and knowledge of John Paul II's wisdom is due

---

[2]   FACTS, accessed October 21, 2020, http://factsaboutfertility.org/.

to my friendship with Breanna and her passion for discovering and teaching the truth about the body and the goodness of God's creation.

Breanna's wisdom about the theology of our bodies as women and the biological science behind our fertility continues to be an incredible resource for me and the women she serves.

If you've ever wanted to learn more about the how and the why behind your fertility as a woman, sister, this letter is for you.

Dear sister,

Progesterone, estrogen, testosterone, FSH, LH, PCOS, amenorrhea . . . it didn't take long in my quest for the truth about my body before I found myself swimming in a pool of "medical lingo" that left me more confused than I was before I started.

I had always been fascinated with the human body, especially regarding fertility and pregnancy. In fact, I'm pretty sure when I was growing up, all my "adventures" with Polly Pockets and Barbies always involved one of them being pregnant and going into labor with "Ken on the way to save her." At an early age, God put the desire in my heart to unwrap the mystery of the woman's ability to conceive another human being. With it also came my greatest fear that pregnancy may never become a reality I'd get to experience.

When I was in late middle school and high school, I was lucky to have a period twice a year. Knowing this couldn't be healthy, I went to countless doctors, who all attributed it to my being very physically active in sports. They would put me on birth control and send me on my way. It wasn't until I got to college that I started to question this: "Birth control is their treatment to help me have periods, because I'm not ovulating, but I'm still not ovulating. How is this 'treating' anything?"

After more diagnoses, lab pokes, and shed tears, I began to feel hopeless. I started to wonder what the truth about my body was. Doctors couldn't tell me, and I knew that couldn't be normal. Would I ever find an answer? I began to wonder if I was made broken and if God had abandoned me on this.

Psalm 34 tells us that the Lord hears the cry of the poor. It was right after this desolation that God started opening doors. I had randomly met two nurses in their forties who listened to my health issues and told me all about a program called the Creighton Model FertilityCare System. It was everything I was looking for. I immediately contacted a FertilityCare practitioner who taught me about the woman's body, how it was supposed to work, and how to read and chart my biological markers.

We soon discovered that I had a lot of medical red flags that needed to be treated. I was then referred to a medical doctor who had special training to read my chart and diagnose and treat my condition, which we later concluded was a severe case of polycystic ovary syndrome. My case was severe enough that it required surgery to fix the problem, which I underwent at the Pope Paul VI Institute three months before I got married. While my body will never be perfect this side of the grave, I can happily say that for the first time in my life, I am able to ovulate on my own, and my PMS has significantly improved. Because of this persistent search for the truth about my body, I am now a labor and delivery nurse, a FertilityCare practitioner, and most importantly, a mother of Kolbe Jude (a beloved soul) and a seven-month-old named Ellis Kapaun.

As St. John Paul II elaborates in his work *Theology of the Body*, the woman's body is both physically and spiritually designed to receive life. When health or circumstances prevent this, it may be very painful and confusing. I vividly remember in the middle of the night, sobbing on my knees in front of the tabernacle, praying, "Lord, this wound of infertility is too deep, too painful. You knew this. Why would you strike me in the most tender part of my heart?" I was spiritually empty at this point; the womb of my soul carried no life. By far, this hurt more than any physical agony that I'd experienced. It was only through Christ's tender, nail-scarred hands wrapping around my heart that I finally opened my soul again to receive the life we are all meant to carry: God's Love. Unworthy as I was, he also decided to heal me physically by allowing the healthy birth of my full-term son.

Now as a FertilityCare practitioner, I have the honor of teaching women and couples about the epitome of God's creation: the design of their bodies and God's plan for them. I empower women by teaching them to read the fertility and health signs their bodies are telling them. I help heal the hurting from the inside out, helping to treat anything from severe PMS to recovering from the devastation of a miscarriage.

For those of you who are searching for answers about your body, never give up! There are people out there who can help you; it's just a matter of finding the right ones. For those of you who have not been educated on how your body naturally works, find somebody who can teach you. God placed an unquenchable desire for truth in our hearts.

"For every one who asks receives, and he who seeks finds, and to him who knocks it will be opened" (Mt 7:8).

Breanna

Breanna McLemore currently works as a registered nurse at Citizen's Medical Center in Colby, KS. She is a Creighton Model FertilityCare practitioner who has been teaching the system since 2015.

Having a passion for ministry, Breanna worked as a campus minister at St. Isidore's Catholic Student Center in Manhattan, KS. There she gained experience teaching classes to college students on St. John Paul II's Love & Responsibility and Theology of the Body.

Breanna is especially passionate about teaching young women and couples how their bodies really work regarding fertility! She also loves the women's health side of the system and is passionate about helping women receive treatment for issues such as PMS, PCOS, infertility, etc. She lives with her husband, Brandon, and son, Ellis, in Colby, KS.

Questions for Reflection

1. What has your own journey to discover the truth about your body and your fertility looked like? Have there been moments where you've felt abandoned or hopeless?

2. What is God desiring to reveal to you about himself as you discover more about the way that he has created and designed your body as a woman?

3. Where and how is God inviting you to carry his love?

Questions for Conversation

1. Have you ever considered that your body is a gift? Or has the search for the truth about the way that your body works looked more like carrying a cross or burden?

2. If your fertility doesn't look like what you expected, what are ways that you can discover healing—physically, emotionally, and spiritually?

3. Are there women in your life who encourage you to discover more about the way that God created your body? How does their witness and accompaniment bring joy and hope into your life?

Come Holy Spirit, living in Mary. Fill me with knowledge and wisdom as I seek to understand, appreciate, and be in awe of the way you've created my body, my whole body. Grant me the grace of receptivity to be open to your life in my soul and to bear the fruit of your love in the world. Amen.

A Letter to the Woman Wondering How to Share Her Faith

"God is opening before the Church the horizons of a humanity more fully prepared for the sowing of the Gospel. I sense that the moment has come to commit all of the Church's energies to a new evangelization and to the mission ad gentes. No believer in Christ, no institution of the Church can avoid this supreme duty: to proclaim Christ to all peoples."

—Pope St. John Paul II

Who comes to mind when you think of someone sharing their faith? Maybe you think of a theology teacher, who went to school to learn about Catholicism. Or perhaps a priest or religious sister comes to mind. People seem to be drawn to them, and sharing their faith is an integral part of their vocation. But does your own story come to mind? Do you share your faith?

You might be hesitant to talk about the Lord with others because you feel like you're underqualified. What if someone asks a question you don't know the answer for? Or maybe you shy away from evangelization because you wonder if it's your job. Isn't it for the people who have those theology degrees or a consecrated vocation? Or maybe you don't have those conversations with others because you're exhausted. I get it, I'm busy too.

But evangelization isn't something to do. Instead, like the feminine genius, it's a way of life. This evangelization centered way of life is something that Tracie has totally embraced. I first met Tracie during the summer of 2015 when I served on staff for a summer mission in western Kansas. We were on ladders, scraping and painting a house together. Her joy and laughter bubbled up and over into our conversation and cheered on anyone who interacted with her.

Through the years that I've been blessed to call her a friend, I've seen her witness the incredible joy of the Gospel to students on college campuses. Every time she calls to catch me up on her mission to know, see, and love the students she evangelizes, I can continue to hear that same infectious joy.

If you're wondering how to share your faith, sister, this letter is for you.

Dear sister,

I'm not writing this letter to give you the magic formula on how to bring others to Christ. I'm not even going to attempt to try to motivate you. The purpose of this letter is not to bore you with all my success stories or burden you with all my failures. There is an abundance of books, videos, and talks about Catholicism that can equip and inspire you to share the faith. I just want to be real about what is going on in my heart as I attempt to make God and his mission of inspiring other disciples the center of my life.

I surmise, if you're reading this, that you've made some commitment to live your life for God. You have turned away from yourself and made a resolution to change your life towards Christ. No doubt, you have experienced a conversion of heart after an encounter with Jesus that caused you to respond to Jesus's invitation to be faithful. I, too, have had many moments of conversion since high school.

Growing up, I went to Catholic school, attended conferences, and experienced mission trips. These were all small encounters that began my journey and choice to be a disciple of Christ.

However, shortly into college, I realized that God calls us (me) to do and be more. He calls us to not just be faithful but fruitful (see Jn 15:8). This invitation is intimidating to say the least. Yet it has been one of my greatest adventures! To bring Jesus into the center of one's life is also to bring his entire mission of drawing all people to his Father (see Jn 6:40).

This poses the challenge that if you have accepted the invitation to have a personal, intimate relationship with Christ through discipleship, are you willing to share his message, the Gospel, with others (see Mt 28:19–20)?

Praying that you have said yes to this (or at least maybe), let me begin to share with you how the Holy Spirit has made this happen, because the Holy Spirit is the chief evangelizer, and not even my incredible charm and humor (I say that humbly of course) can bring the most hardened hearts to Jesus. The bottom line is that it is all Jesus (see Jn 15:5).

Before I could share his message, the Gospel, I had to recognize the need for it in my life and in others. If part of this message is that we are made for a relationship (see CCC 1), where was this void in my life?

I felt this emptiness in friendships, friendships with other women who wanted to be disciples. Sometimes my discipleship left me feeling isolated and alone in my constant grind to become a saint. I think this is the reason I love the raw honesty of Martha, "Lord, do you not care that my sister has left me to serve alone? Tell her then to help me" (Lk 10:40). This is often me crying out when trying to share the Gospel.

I had to come to this conclusion: everyone needs to be invested in, to be loved, known, and cared for whether they know it or not. So whether it is the girls that show up to my Bible study every week or the friend that has shut out God in every way, everyone has this desire. They need it because they were created for it.

Sharing one's faith starts with simply developing a friendship founded on trust. After I accepted God's call to cultivate real relationships with others, I had to recognize the brokenness in the world.

You might be laughing, thinking, "Oh, I know how hard life is. I do not have to go looking for it." That is fair. Life is hard. However, at some point, all of us either ignore, become numb, or do not care we are broken. I was broken by sin, suffering, and my own limitations.

Once I figured out and accepted that, I was ready to acknowledge that I needed a savior. Leading others to Christ means we have to allow them to see their own weakness so they can see the need for a relationship with God. And it is through that deep and personal relationship that we receive grace.

And while this seems easier said than done, it is actually the greatest of news because we have a God that is close to the brokenhearted (see Ps 34:19)! We have a God that became human to experience similar brokenness so he could be near and compassionate toward us.

Being a disciple is challenging, complicated, and exhilarating. It is by grace that the foundation of trust is built. You have to be willing to ask probing but not intrusive questions, be steadfast in support during times of trial and tribulation, and be vulnerable in allowing others to witness their own messes as well as your own. Soon a relationship begins to take shape and thrive. And God is at the core of it all.

This next part is where the fun begins. This is when God can start to really work in everyone's hearts! I have seen it over and over again on college campuses as a missionary and in the lives of many of my friends. When I said yes to God's will and committed to being in a relationship with him, God started to give me the grace to be more like him and to live a life of adventure and fullness!

Consequently, this is when we all can fully accompany others into the life of the Church. This invitation includes not only Christ-filled friendships but also a church community that is not defined by or confined to chapels and/or churches but rather one which thrives in the reality of everyday living.

Conversions can happen on the floor of a bedroom, at a kitchen table, a volleyball court, or even in a bar. I challenge all of you women who want to share your faith to build relationships fueled by God's grace in places big and small, easy and hard, and common and unique.

Do not fret that you do not know how. The Holy Spirit will be your guide. You just need to show up with an open heart, a heart immersed in grace!

Tracie Lynn Thiabult,
FOCUS missionary

Tracie Thibault grew up on the Great Plains of Kansas with three older sisters playing sports, learning how to perform prose from her mom, and gardening with her dad. Her love of serving the poor and sick in high school and college inspired her abroad and to local mission efforts. Although her plan was to attend Optometry school immediately after graduating from Kansas State University with a degree in biology, God called her to serve for two years of mission on college campuses through FOCUS (Fellowship of Catholic University Students). While being assigned to Louisiana State University and the University of Alabama, she served as a campus outreach missionary evangelizing through Bible studies, retreats, one-on-one discipleships, and mission trips with collegiate athletes. She will be pursuing a doctorate in optometry in Memphis, Tennessee and sharing the Gospel with her new classmates. Tracie's goal is to own her own optometry practice that promotes Catholic values and service to the physically poor.

Questions for Reflection

1. What fears are holding you back from sharing Christ with people in your life?
2. Where is a place in your life where you're wounded, and how has the Lord transformed and redeemed that area of brokenness?
3. Who are three people in your life that God is inviting you to dive into meaningful friendship with?

Questions for Conversation:

1. Who is someone who has shared their faith with you, and how has their witness impacted your own relationship with the Lord?

2. What is one practical way that you can begin to live evangelization as a way of life?

3. It's tempting to think that sharing your faith requires packing your bags and going to some far-off place. But, like St. Teresa of Calcutta encouraged us, we have to "find our own Calcutta." Where is your mission field?

Come Holy Spirit, living in Mary. Bring your boldness, passion, and courage so that I can invite others to join me on this journey back to the Sacred Heart of Jesus. Guide me into the conversations where you desire to speak your truth into the lives of those I encounter. Open my heart to receive your grace. Amen.

A Letter to the Woman Witnessing to the Joy of Christ

"Do not be afraid of holiness. It will take away none of your energy, vitality or joy. On the contrary, you will become what the Father had in mind when he created you, and you will be faithful to your deepest self."
—Pope Francis

Do you think you're not enough to share the Gospel and joy of Christ with others in your life? Are you worried that you're not good enough, smart enough, holy enough, extroverted, or joyful enough?

If those lies have haunted your heart, you're not alone. I've struggled with those feelings too. When I'm battling those lies straight from the devil and desiring instead to lean into the truth that God says about me and to grow in joy with him, I look to a woman in my life whose joy is contagious.

Sarah's laughter and smile reveal to me the reality of what it is like to live fully alive and free in the joy of Christ. She truly has become a big sister to me. We've prayed, hiked, sang, and drunk countless cups of coffee together. Her friendship on this journey to heaven is a godsend in my life.

If you are wondering how you can witness to the joy of Christ in your daily life, sister, this letter is for you.

Dear sister,

I wish we could be together to have this conversation! I imagine us by the fireside on a cold day, curled up with hot tea and enjoying the stillness of nature so particular to winter. But since that isn't the case, I pray that this letter will bring you encouragement and strength both in your precious and unique identity and in your capability to bring the joy of the Gospel to others.

It can be easy to find ourselves thinking about "evangelization" as a very complicated thing requiring degrees and lectures and how-to manuals. But when we think that way, it's also easy to become overwhelmed and full of self-doubt, making statements like "I don't have all the answers" or "I'm not engaging, smart, charismatic, etc. enough to evangelize." Evangelization then becomes an anxious activity when it can actually be a very simple and natural way of life rooted in the witness of the nativity scene. Let me explain.

Our Father made us, like the star of Bethlehem, to be beacons of light in this world. You are your own unique kind of light—you may sing with abandon or you may speak powerfully in more silent ways. But while we all express our light uniquely, we are all made ultimately for love, and love pours itself out, just as a star pours out its rays of light on the earth.

We are called by our Father to be beacons of hope, to be stars of witness to his Son—to the truth of God with us.

Contemplate, for a moment, the story of the Magi and their arrival at Bethlehem.

The Father, in the great poetry of creation, wrote the good news of the birth of his Son into movement of the stars. He placed this one particular star, this guiding light, in the sky.

The Magi—struck by beauty and the message it related—responded. They followed the light of the Lord, and this light led them all the way to Bethlehem.

The star itself said not a word, and yet the hearts of the Magi were moved enough to take a dark and uncertain journey towards conversion, towards Christ.

More surprisingly, once the Magi arrived, Jesus said not a word.

But even without words, do we doubt the conversion of the hearts of the Magi? Do we doubt their real adoration of the God made man? We may ask ourselves: why did Jesus decide to bring them to himself at this point when he was so vulnerable, so helpless, when he in his humanity was incapable of apologetics or discourses? Why didn't he choose to bring them to himself when he was older, capable of convincing with words? What is Jesus communicating to us in this moment of deep encounter with the Magi—an encounter in which the primary movers are a star and a baby, both of which are silent?

I think Jesus is showing us vividly that evangelization is rooted in encounter and that the most powerful thing about evangelization may not always be the words spoken. Consider, rather, the light in one's glance, the kindness in a smile, the grace in a helping hand.

Perhaps, at its core, evangelization is the vulnerability of allowing people to encounter the reality and joy of who you are and the Presence you contain. While this will often include conversation, it will always require love, and this is what I suggest returning to when feeling overwhelmed or inadequate.

Isn't this a freeing thought? With or without words, you are always capable of sharing the gift of light, love, and joy. You are always capable of sharing the One you love, the One who always lives in the truest center of your heart.

You are always capable, and you are always called.

Think about the nature and mission of the stars: to burn and share their light with the universe. For them to hold back their light is not possible, it is not within their nature. Likewise, when we live in the freedom of the children of God, we are living out our truest self, and our light pours out. We are in harmony with who we are and for whom we were made. Our nature and our mission are one.

You see, there is no need to be afraid. Your Father calls you only to that for which he has already made you!

We have a beautiful, strong, feminine model of this evangelization which flows out of "being"—a woman who has very few words recorded in Scripture but who nevertheless brought Christ to the world more powerfully than any of us ever can! I was struck by this when I was praying with the Litany of Loreto, an old prayer of the Church in honor of Mary.

Refuge of sinners, pray for us.
Comforter of the afflicted, pray for us.
Help of Christians, pray for us.

Mary, in many of her titles, shows us in these very salutations how we can witness to the joy and love of the Gospel, to the joy and love of what it means to be a Christian:

Refuge of sinners – Am I a gentle and welcoming presence to my struggling brothers and sisters?

Comforter of the afflicted – Am I reaching out to those with heavy burdens?

Help of Christians – Am I available?

Our Lady of the Smile – Am I conscious of my demeanor to others? Am I witnessing the joy I hold inside?

Mary, Undoer of Knots – Am I praying, recognizing that prayer is essential to the heart of evangelization? Am I praying for knots to be untied, obstacles to be removed in the faith walks of others?

Remember that evangelization, at its core, is not teaching, is not preaching; while these are very important, evangelization is first and foremost sharing the light and joy of God with us, often in the simple, everyday moments and actions of life. Start here and the rest will come as God wills and as you grow. Share who you are and who he is in you—be not afraid!

Mary, Star of the New Evangelization, pray for us.

In his heart,

Sarah

Sarah Burns is a Catholic woman who tries her best to live out the words of St. Irenaeus that "the glory of God is a man fully alive." She has a background in art, music, literature, and ministry. Her love for mountains and books takes a back seat only to her love for Jesus and people. Often found on the trails on warm sunny days, and curled up with a book and a hot drink on the cold and rainy ones, she tries to follow Jesus wherever he leads.

Questions for Reflection

1. What is your unique witness to the Lord? How is he calling you specifically to share the love of the Gospel?
2. Do you worry that you will not have all the words or answers to witness to the beauty of the Catholic faith? Which example of a silent character in the story of the Nativity strikes you, and why?
3. Is your prayer life the source and heart of your desire to evangelize? Have you asked the Lord how he desires to share his joy with others?

Questions for Conversation

1. What are some aspects of evangelization that have caused you anxiety about sharing your faith? How can Mary's example of being instead of doing change the way you approach opportunities to share your faith?
2. Is there a certain title of Our Lady that you are drawn to in your personal devotion? How has she taught you what it means to be a Christian?
3. How can you be a witness to the joy of Christ as you interact with others in your daily life?

Come Holy Spirit, living in Mary. Remove the fears and obstacles that hold me back from proclaiming the joy and love of the Gospel. Let my life be a joyful witness to the hope that comes from trusting you with everything. Help me be attuned to the simple ways that you desire to work in and through me. Amen.

A Letter to the Woman Growing Closer to Our Lady

"In dangers, in doubts, in difficulties, think of Mary, call upon Mary. Let not her name depart from your lips, never suffer it to leave your heart. And that you may obtain the assistance of her prayer, neglect not to walk in her footsteps. With her for guide, you shall never go astray; while invoking her, you shall never lose heart; so long as she is in your mind, you are safe from deception; while she holds your hand, you cannot fall; under her protection you have nothing to fear; if she walks before you, you shall not grow weary; if she shows you favor, you shall reach the goal."

—St. Bernard of Clairvaux

Each woman lives out the feminine genius in a beautifully unique way, but one woman lives out the feminine genius to its absolute fullest, and that's Our Lady. Her constant yes to the Lord is the ultimate exemplar of receptivity. Her beautiful, giving heart shows us how to be generous. Her awareness of the needs of others is an example of feminine sensitivity. She lives out physical maternity through the birth of the Lord and is a model for spiritual maternity since she sees each and every one of us as her children.

But when I struggle to live out the feminine genius in my own life, when I stumble along the path to holiness, a relationship and friendship with Our Lady can seem intimidating and impossible. There have been seasons in my life when even though I desire to grow close to the Blessed Mother, I don't know how to take the first steps.

Jacque is a woman in my life who has taught me so much about getting to know Mary better. To say that Jacque loves Our Lady is an understatement. Jacque is a woman who has an incredibly beautiful, special, and fervent love for Mary. Her relationship with Mary has changed her life and given her the courage to say yes to God and strive to become the woman that he has created her to be. But Jacque didn't always have a relationship with Mary, which is why her story of growing in that relationship has inspired me in moments when I wonder how to begin to grow in friendship with the Mother of God.

If you're wanting to grow in your relationship with the Blessed Mother but don't know where to start, sister, this letter is for you.

Dear sister,

"I don't even want to be Catholic anymore," I messaged my friend one day while sitting in the halls of Franciscan University, one of the most Catholic universities in the United States. I was a freshman in college, and seeped in the thick mud of depression, anxiety, disordered eating, and repressed trauma, I felt totally and utterly alienated from God and his love. I wondered if he even existed. For the next two years, I struggled to stay afloat in the storm of depression and anxiety. In my attempts to cope, I fell further and further into the trenches of sin. I would run to confession from time to time out of the fear that hell might exist, but my heart felt numb and cold. I often missed Mass and rarely felt even the smallest lick of guilt.

Looking back, I realize God was slowly and gently making himself known to me. During my junior year of college, the opportunity to join Franciscan University's Women's Ministry arose. Motivated by the desire to beef up my resume, I interviewed to join. Surprisingly, I was accepted, and so began my long journey back into the faith. I quickly befriended Sister Anna Rose, the supervisor of Women's Ministry, and through conversations with her, the desire to grow closer to God began slowly burning in my heart. As weak as the flames were, I started to think that maybe, just maybe, God had not abandoned me. Maybe, just maybe, he wanted me to be a saint too and be with him in heaven one day.

That following summer, a friend gifted me with a rosary bracelet. I hadn't prayed the Rosary on my own in years, and I actually dreaded it when I was forced to pray it in groups. But for some reason, I wore the bracelet everywhere. I was raised Catholic, but I am embarrassed to say that, at the time, I could not properly pray the Rosary by myself. So, in waves of anxiety and depression, I clung to those beads, repeating Hail Marys in my head to hold on to my sanity. It was in these desperate moments that Our Blessed Mother gently carved a place in my heart. I began calling her

"Mama" or "Mom" in my head when thinking of her (which I had thought was bizarre and off-putting before).

My senior year at Franciscan, I felt a soft and gentle tug on my heart from the Blessed Mother to join Totus Tuus, Maria household, which means Totally Yours, Mary—St. John Paul II's motto for his papacy. As a part of that household, I consecrated myself to Jesus through Mary using Louis de Monfort's model for Marian consecration. During consecration, a fiery, passionate, and deep love for Jesus was ignited in my heart. My once cold and numb heart felt as if it was bleeding for Jesus. I had never felt his love for me so strongly, and all I wanted was to be in the presence of the Eucharist. I often found myself weeping before the Eucharist, overcome by his love for me and my love for him. And I know that is because of Our Blessed Mother.

Mary's main goal is to bring us to Jesus and bring Jesus to us, just as she brought him to the world in her womb when she said yes to God in humble service. Mary is my mother, she is your mother, and she longs to bring us to her Son. The only person I love more than my sweet Mama is Jesus, and that is exactly how she wants it.

Now, Mary is not only an integral part of my prayer life but an essential part of my very breath, my very being. She is the sweet mother who is a beacon of the Lord's mercy to me. When I run away, when I trip and fall into the mud of sin and despair, she comes to me and gently pulls me from the dirt. She wipes away the mud and blood from my face, clothes me in her mantle, and gently leads me back to her Son, whispering over and over in my ear, "It's okay, honey.

Let's just get you cleaned up and make our way back. It's okay. We just have to walk back. I have you. Don't worry."

She is the star that never leaves me, the presence that is always by my side, guiding me over and over back to her Son when I run.

You may be wondering, "Why do we need Mary? Why can't we just go straight to Jesus?" The best explanation I've ever heard is that because God used Mary to bring Jesus to this earth through her womb, he continues to use her to bring lost souls to her Son under her mantle.

I am so, so thankful for the gift of this sweet mother in my life. Through her, Jesus came for me. he came for me in my darkness and in my despair, and he used his gentle and sweet mother to guide me back to him

Dear sisters, when you feel lost, broken, and distant from the Lord, call on our Blessed Mother. She is always waiting to wrap us in her tender care and walk hand in hand, side by side, and back to her Son.

Jacque

Jacque Anderson currently resides in Chicago where she works for Aid for Women, a nonprofit that serves women in crisis pregnancies. A graduate of Franciscan University of Steubenville, Jacque is passionate about writing and speaking on faith, ministry, and mental health in order to shed light in areas often laced with shame to cultivate healing and freedom. She enjoys running, coffee with friends, reading, and photography. You can learn more about her on her website www.jacquelynanderson.com and listen to her speak on her two podcasts Entrust Me Here *and* Let's Talk About It with Jacque and Megan.

Questions for Reflection

1. What is your relationship with Our Lady like? Does she feel distant and untouchable, close and dear, or somewhere in between?
2. Is Christ inviting you to get to know his mother better in this season of your life? What does that invitation look like for you?
3. Are there parts of your story where you feel lost or broken? Have you asked Our Lady to help you back to the heart of Jesus, her Son?

Questions for Conversation

1. Have you ever consecrated yourself to Our Lady? If you have, did you notice any changes in your prayer life or the way you interacted with others after you made your consecration?
2. How is Our Lady bringing Christ into your life?
3. Our Lady responded with a Fiat, her joyful and receptive yes to God's plan in her life. Where in your own life is Christ inviting you to say yes, and how can Our Lady help you be open to God's will?

Come Holy Spirit, living in Mary. Just as you filled Our Lady with the grace and peace to give a Fiat that resounds throughout all of salvation history, help me to give my own yes to the plans that you have in store for me. When I'm tempted to question your plans or your goodness, help me turn to Our Lady as my heavenly mother whose only desire is to see me grow closer in unity with her Son and his will for my life. Amen.

A Letter to the Woman in a Season of Conversion

"Conversion is a gift of God, a work of the Blessed Trinity."
—Pope St. John Paul II

What's your conversion story? Maybe you're a woman who has found her home in the Catholic Church after a long season of searching. Maybe you, like me, are a cradle Catholic and your life is full of small conversions, times where you've made active decisions to grow deeper in your relationship with Christ and his Catholic Church. Or perhaps you're still in the process of discovering the person of Christ and the Church that he founded.

Regardless of where you are on the road of conversion, you have a story to tell. Christ is working in your life, weaving together events, people, and places to form the story of how you discover him and delight in his goodness. It's tempting to think you don't have a conversion story, especially if your conversion takes place in quiet moments, instead of St. Paul style life-altering events. But every single one of us has a unique journey to encountering the truth, goodness, and beauty of God.

If there's a woman in my life who has lit a fire underneath me to dive into conversations about Scripture and my own life of conversion, it's Sonja Corbitt. She's the perfect guide for this conversation about making changes in our life so that we can become more like Christ, and more of the women he's created us to be.

Whether it's through conversations with Sonja, reading her books, or listening to her podcasts in the early hours of the morning during my prayer time, I'm in awe of her knowledge of Scripture and her relationship with the Lord. I've been blessed to meet Sonja face to face during a local women's retreat a few years ago, and she's just as fierce, authentic, and genuine in person as she is in her writing and podcasts.

If you're in the process of turning back to the heart of the Father, sister, this letter is for you.

Dear sister,

I was coming out. The Southern Baptist Bible teacher in me was terrified by the impending revelation I was about to break to my husband that I was going to a Catholic Mass. He was on the lawn mower and surely startled at seeing me in a dress on Saturday afternoon. He pulled up and cut the motor with a question on his face.

"I'm going to Mass," I threw out like a dare, albeit a mousey one. Distaste wrinkled his brow when he shot back, "What? Are you gonna be a little Catholic girl, now?" At that moment, I decided to let my freak flag fly. You know when something leaps out of your mouth and you appreciate its terrifyingly brilliant pithiness afterward? That's how

I felt later, remembering my expression of (purely humble) rebuke when I replied, "Are you persecuting me?"

My satisfaction at his shocked Holy-Spirit-conviction face lasted only long enough for me to escape the driveway, and my twenty-minute trip to the church was wrought with doubt. "Too late now!" my mind indicted.

A year earlier, a member of my Baptist Sunday School class entered the Church at the Easter Vigil and asked me to attend. I thought it was the weirdest service I had ever sat through and that we would all likely go to hell. And now, here I was, headed to Mass for myself.

I had a father wound that provoked behaviors that God consistently confronted and corrected over the course of my twenties. So when our evangelical church split twice under the sniping of a few notorious members, devastating the congregation and both pastors, I saw the rebellion for what it was. I also knew the Bible well enough to know that God had made better provision for his pastors and people. I began searching for something less protest-anty.

Over the course of a year, I surreptitiously read my way through the early Church Fathers, the Catechism, scores of encyclicals and council documents, and annals of apologetics material, attempting to integrate the most difficult teachings into my previous education and understanding. But that Saturday afternoon was the day I stepped publicly into the most difficult season of my entire life.

I had grown up hearing from the pulpit, and even teaching myself, that the Catholic Church was a cult, the Whore of Babylon in Revelation 17, with the pope as her False Prophet (see Rv 13). Anti-Catholic teaching was the eschatological milk we were brought up on as Southern evangelicals in those days, and the views are not much improved now. Most of my Baptist friends pretended not to see me at the grocery store and fled. My denominational publisher dropped me, and I didn't blame them. "Well-meaning" coworkers—bless their hearts—likened me to Eve and chastised my husband for allowing me to lead our family to hell all over again.

Furthermore, I had just begun to enjoy some local credibility as an "anointed" Christian speaker and author in my denomination. I was receiving multiple invitations to speak, to interview with the evangelical Christian TV station, and my first Bible study was about to be published. And here I was throwing it all away on a summer Saturday for the hope of the Eucharist I couldn't receive for another nine months.

My husband and I couldn't speak Catholic without arguing. Although neglecting to set foot in a church for a decade and a half, my parents lamented that I was turning my back on everything I had been taught. They threw out anti-Catholic questions that were really statements-thou-shalt-not-argue-with, as though I hadn't asked myself all those indignant questions and reassured myself with the answers a hundred or more times already.

In fact, for a long time after my conversion, I would suddenly freeze with doubt on a biblical interpretation, argue vociferously against the Catholic position in my head, and then rebut my own arguments in mental ping pong until relief dawned all over again that Catholicism is true!

Adding to our grief, the autumn I came into the Church, I was postpartum, my oldest child had a devastating accident that almost killed him and left him an invalid for months, and my pastor displaced two beloved, long-serving volunteers in making me the paid religious education director, to the horror of our entire parish—especially the seminarian who stalked me until I took legal action. His sudden removal seemed to solidify the parish's hatred for the upstart Protestant girl without a Catholic clue in her head.

I continued dropping Sunday dinner in the crock pot before attending vigil Mass every Saturday, and then went to the Baptist church on Sunday to lend as much normalcy as possible to our family's reputation and Sunday routine.

Meanwhile, my family pitied me, my friends shunned me, my enemies ridiculed me, my denomination abandoned me, my parish abhorred me, I feared divorce, I was caring for an invalid and a nursing infant, and I held a part-time job serving a parish that despised me, all while battling postpartum hormones. I clung to daily assurance in the Scriptures that Mary was my model and I was exactly where God wanted me through all of it. She encouraged me to be silent and soft, to refrain from defending myself, and to wait for God's vindication.

Months later, my husband and I were taking our customary Sunday afternoon walk together. I felt sorry for the tension between us and the fear and embarrassment he was enduring. I didn't look at him when I said, "You know, honey, you remind me of Joseph." He stopped in the middle of the street and looked at me with shock. "What did you say?"

"You remind me of Joseph?" I repeated, unsure if I should.

"You're not going to believe what happened to me this morning." He meant while the kids and I were at Mass, since he had stopped going to church altogether. He went on with gathering excitement. "I was sitting on the toilet this morning and God said to me, plain as day, 'You are Joseph.'"

It was my turn to be shocked. That was the first of several interventions that the Lord worked on my behalf with those who had judged me. Our bishop removed the stalking seminarian, and after having experienced two evangelical church rebellions, my husband witnessed how legitimate church authority is meant to operate. We did a "two-fer" (that's "two-for-the-price-of-one" in Southern) when our sons were baptized together. He warily attended their baptisms, because Catholic. Three to one.

Five years later, I asked him to video the RCIA classes I had been teaching using a Catholic faith-sharing curriculum I wrote and that later became a published best-seller. He entered the Church the next Easter Vigil, and now I am the Bible Study Evangelista.

If you are in a season of conversion, resist defending yourself, lean into the darkness and difficulty, and wait it out with Our Lady, trusting his promise with her: "No weapon that is fashioned against you shall prosper, and you shall confute every tongue that rises against you in judgment. This is the heritage of the servants of the LORD and their vindication from me, says the LORD" (Is 54:17).

Dear persecuted woman, hide and wait, because when God defends you, you have been unequivocally defended.

Sonja

Sonja Corbitt is the Bible Study Evangelista - a best-selling author, weekly Catholic TV and radio show host, and creator of the LOVE the Word® Bible study method and journal.

Questions for Reflection

1. What is your conversion story?
2. Do you see God as your heavenly Father, a Father who defends you? If not, how does he desire to heal the father wound in your heart?
3. How is the Lord inviting you right now into a deeper relationship with him, a step further into this life of conversion?

Questions for Conversation

1. Have you ever shared your conversion story with others? What has kept you back from witnessing to the unique way that God is calling your heart back to his?
2. Mary gives us a beautiful example of what it means to silently ponder what she observes in her heart. Do you find this silence and pondering easy to do in your daily life, or is it a challenge to incorporate this kind of contemplation?
3. Have your ever been persecuted in your faith? What strengthens you in your beliefs when others question what you know to be true?

Come Holy Spirit, living in Mary. Give me a spirit of courage as I continue to journey back to the Lord and his Catholic Church. Grant me conviction for your truth, humility in the face of confrontation, and the wisdom of knowing that you seek after me and call me home. Amen.

A Letter to the Woman Facing the Unexpected

"The Spirit is the gift of God, of this God, our Father, who always surprises us: the God of surprises, because he is a living God, a God who abides in us, a God who moves our heart, a God who is in the Church and walks with us; and he always surprises us on this path."

—Pope Francis

When you go through an unexpected change or struggle, you may find yourself thinking about life in terms of "before" and "after." I know in my story, there are many markers of these "befores" and "afters." When Alexa reflects on her journey, she remembers her life before and after February 17, 2017, when she found out she was expecting a baby girl.

Sharing our unique stories can help others realize that they are not alone in this struggle of unexpected challenges. Each one of us has our own unique story of joy and struggle. We all have our own "Februaries." So how do we be brave and face that struggle head on? Alexa is a woman who I have long admired for how she is leading the way with a conversation about beauty, meaning, conversation, and community. We're all facing our own February, or we have one that is yet to come.

If you're facing an unexpected challenge and need reassurance and to know you're not alone, sister, this letter is for you.

Dear sister,

It was a rainy February day in LA, and within minutes of a quick trip to CVS, I found out I'd be a mother. I was twenty-three, single, and so full of fear. I went from standing with the world at my feet to falling humbly to my knees. The life I'd woven for myself unraveled in seconds. And in the same breath, it was the moment when my life's most beautiful journey began.

In the months that followed, I grieved. I grieved the life I thought I'd have, the freedom I knew I was giving up; I grieved the selfishness I didn't want to let go of just yet. Little by little, I let go of each thing and replaced each one with something new. A new humility long overdue, a new self-love for my resilience and strength, a new realization of my limitations and so the sacrifice of my self-reliance. With every little thing I let go, there was a struggle in the change. There was a game of tug-of-war within me. But with every release, I felt something much greater take its place.

When my daughter, Renley, was born, my heart changed instantly. When I looked into her eyes for the first time, I understood God's love for the first time. It was love without contingencies, freedom where control was absent, acceptance without a "but." I began to see myself as Renley saw me: lovable, deserving, enough. Even on my hardest days, her love brought me healing and joy. She was and always will be the thing I needed. For a long time, I thought it was motherhood that healed me, but that wasn't quite it; it was love.

Looking back now, as almost three years have passed since that rainy day in February, I see how different my life looks compared to the one I envisioned then. And the one I have now feels so much fuller because of Renley's life. It sounds morbid, but there is a dying to self when a woman becomes a mother, and yet just as Jesus promises, in that death, there is new life. I was able to experience what happens when we trust in that promise for a resurrection. I experienced the freedom and the joy in letting go; in fact, it hurt so much more to keep holding onto my plans, my expectations, and what I wanted. Instead of the way I envisioned, my life is fuller. I see beauty in the little things. My daughter teaches me every day to become more like a child. I have suffered and come to understand my suffering, and with it, I can be more present in the suffering of others.

That's what change and suffering do. They not only change our realities from the outside, but they change us interiorly, and in my experience, always in ways we needed changing. Stagnancy is worth fearing, not change. And I just think to myself now: run to it. As my boss would say, "run to the thing that makes you most afraid, because there's growth there." God continuously calls us to go deeper; he never says, "Your work is done here." Instead, he leads us through a lifetime of growing, of forgiving ourselves, of learning to let him love us in our pain and showing us there is hope when we feel hopeless. He teaches us how to be love for our friends. He leads us into vulnerability without shame. We bond with him much like the way we bond with our friends when we are vulnerable in an empathetic space. For all of these reasons, I've come to believe there is so much beauty in suffering. Don't get me wrong, I still struggle to trust in its midst, I still make the same mistakes of holding tightly to my self-reliance and trying to heal on my own. But with every season of suffering and letting God into the pain, the world looks brighter because I understand that beauty is a combination of death and new life.

The story of my love for Renley and her love for me is a story that's been repeated in my life. One of God chasing me steadfastly and one of my running steadfastly away. Somehow, for most of my life, I have believed that love must be earned and that one must be perfect in order to receive it. And so, you can imagine, with every mistake, I hold myself hostage. And every time, God holds out his hand with the invitation, "Let me love you in your pain and shower you in my mercy." And so many times I tell him what I told my mother when I was little, "I can do it myself."

As my life continues to change and I continue to evolve, one thing remains consistent: change. Change is inevitable. Whether it's big or small, expected or unexpected, somehow it still picks us up by the ankles and shakes us upside down until every ounce of expectation or control falls from us. Somehow, with every new chapter in my life, I've been shocked by how different the lessons learned were from the ones I expected, as if beforehand I thought I already knew them. With every season of change, I can feel God pulling back another layer of my heart. I can feel him asking me to let him in a little more this time. I can feel myself become more me, the woman he created me to be each time I reach out—hands shaking—before him in prayer and give up the thing I'm clinging to.

And each time, when the clouds clear and the clarity comes, I think to myself, "Remember this moment. All things are passing. Don't fight it so hard next time. Don't cling to your self-reliance. Remove your armor. Open your hands and your heart. Let him in to love and heal."

So, friend, I remind you this day and the next: All things are passing. Don't fight and cling to your self-reliance. Remove your armor. Open your hands and your heart. Let him in.

$\mathcal{A}$lexa

Alexa Hyman is a full-time working mother living in Chicago with her two-year-old daughter, Renley Jane. She is a writer, contributor, and bubble-bath lover. After experiencing her unplanned pregnancy, she became passionate about sharing her own personal experiences in order to make other women feel less alone. When she is not working in financial services, she mentors women who are facing unplanned pregnancies and manages an Instagram community and website called Back in February. You can find her on Instagram at @backinfebruary_ or at BackinFebruary.com.

Questions for Reflection

1. Have you experienced suffering in your life, and have you been able to see the beauty in that suffering?
2. Where in your story has love healed wounds in your heart?

3. Do you have a tendency to cling to self-reliance, to figure out everything on your own? How is God calling you to surrender, and do you trust him enough to let go and give everything over to him?

Questions for Conversation

1. In your relationship with God, have you ever believed that you have to earn his love or that you must be perfect before you can receive the gifts he has in store for you?
2. What does healthy vulnerability with the Lord look like? How can you grow deeper in your communication with God in prayer?
3. What does surrender to change look like in your life? What are some practical ways that you can begin to let go of armor and let God love you and heal you?

Come Holy Spirit, living in Mary. When I'm jolted by unexpected change in my life, give me the grace to let my response be surrender and trust instead of fear and grasping. In moments where things do not go as planned, open my eyes up to your goodness and the beauty of the present moment. Amen.

A Letter to the Woman Looking for Her Place in the Catholic Church

"To be a servant of Christ is to be truly free."
—St. Agatha

Every single person created by God in his image and his likeness is called to holiness—no exceptions. Christ is calling each and every one of us back to his Sacred Heart. He longs for us to grow into the women that he has created us to be.

But if you experience same-sex attraction, you may wonder if you belong here in the Catholic Church, if you have a home here. You might wonder how to bring up your experience of same-sex attraction with friends and family in conversation.

Avera Maria is a woman who is an incredible witness to the reality and the heaviness of carrying a cross of same-sex attraction. She joyfully proclaims the beauty and hope found in Christ and in his Catholic Church. Her wisdom, honesty, and courage are shedding light on today's conversation about being a Catholic who is experiencing same-sex attraction.

If you've longed to find your place within the Church that Christ founded, sister, this letter is for you.

Dear sister,

"She will want to love [another woman] and realize that the Catholic Church may not be for her, but another faith who loves Christ [and] will accept her whole without compromise—unlike the Catholic faith. Once she has had a true darkness of the soul, as I have had, then she will see reason— that Christ never said anything about homosexuality."

This was a comment left under an article that the *National Catholic Register* wrote about me after my open letter to the bishops at the Youth Synod went viral back in October of 2018.

In this letter, I expressed my concern that pro-LGBTQ+ organizations were lobbying for the Church to change her teachings on homosexuality. I know that these good, true, and beautiful teachings can—and should—never change, but I wanted the bishops of the Church to know that there are indeed young people out there who recognize just how incredible and freeing these teachings really are.

Of course, this letter was met with some backlash, like that of this man who was obviously concerned but had missed or misinterpreted the dear Bride of Christ, and why she so boldly professes what she does.

My dear sisters, no matter who you are, what you've done or haven't done, or what your cross is or your struggles are, I assure you, the Church is your home. The good Bride of Christ, our Mother Church, welcomes us as only a mother could and loves us as only a mother can. She pulls us in close and desires our happiness and freedom, and she keeps us safe by pulling back our hands when we place them near to the fires of hell, knowing full well that such fires bring us, her beloved children, harm.

While strict in her teachings, she knows us and knows what is best for us, for her Beloved, our Lord Jesus Christ, knows us and loves us. She loves and accepts the whole of our identity given to us by God and does not compromise but continues to call us to the very heights of holiness, to the heights of heaven. In a whisper, Christ conveys all that he knows and wills for us, and our Mother Church submits to his authority, doing all in her power to protect us under his divine charge.

O what a loving Savior we have, dear sisters! And what a good and gentle mother at his pierced side! Because of him, she sees us through and knows that her Lover wills our good. In this, she commands us to lead lives in truth, in authentic human freedom. These demands that she impresses upon us in her teachings are not without meaning; on the contrary, they are rich in objective truth, in love, in knowledge of the human heart.

Her good and gracious Lover paid the price for our freedom in his Blood, and it was this sacrifice that he bore that saved us and her; knowing full well the price that was paid for our freedom, she fights to keep it by ensuring we do not fall slaves to sin and to death. This is why she teaches what she does. What mother wants to see her child a slave?

Love must always proceed law; in her demands, she first loves, and loves without regard for self. Desiring the good of us, even if we do not, she commands all that she does. What a gift! What a grace! And though, my dear sisters, darkness may threaten to overtake you, to blind you from the reality that both your Lover and our mother stand firm in his love for us, I charge you here and now never to lose trust.

I think back to a beloved children's story, to C. S. Lewis's masterpiece *The Lion, The Witch, and the Wardrobe*, and I recall the words of the Beaver to the children when he and his wife were asked if the great lion Aslan was safe.

"Safe? . . . Who said anything about safe? 'Course he isn't safe. But he's good. He's the king, I tell you."[3]

Ours is not a Lover who promises us safety, my dear sisters. Ours is not a Lover who promises us a life without pain or suffering. But he promises us his very self and the salvation his sacrifice on the cross won for us. Ours is a Lover who has already won the great battle and yet still fights for the love of his beloved, his beloved being each and every one of us.

While it is true, my dear sisters, that Our Lord may not have mentioned anything about homosexuality itself, he mentioned, by his actions, what true love looks like; we see his example of this love when we look above the tabernacle in our churches, looking upon his outstretched arms nailed to the wood of the cross.

This love sought to give, never to take; to give life, never to take or waste it; to will the good of the beloved, not the

---

[3]   C. S. Lewis, *The Lion, the Witch, and the Wardrobe* (New York: HarperCollins, 1994).

desires of the self. This is the love each and every one of us is called to imitate in this life.

I hope and I pray, my dear sisters in Christ, my dear daughters of his Bride the Church, that even in your darkest moments, you will never forget the light of Christ's face. This face is flooded with compassion, with remembrance of his sacrifice, with the desire to remain with you in heaven for all eternity.

Remember that Our Lord's commands are sure (see Ps 118:86) and that he is good and worthy of your trust. He would never withhold anything you need from you, not even his own blood. Ours is a Lover who accepts us whole and does not compromise, not even on his teachings. Ours is the Lover above all lovers; ours is a good and gracious God.

Avera Maria Santos

Avera Maria Santos is a Catholic Speaker and Writer. Since 2017, she has written extensively and traveled the country speaking about her testimony of experiencing same-sex attractions while remaining faithful to Christ and his Bride, the Church. Her written works have been featured in the National Catholic Register, and she has appeared on EWTN'S Life on the Rock, as well as several other Catholic publications and podcasts.

Questions for Reflection

1. Have you ever believed that a part of your story makes you "not enough" or "too much" for the Catholic Church? How does God want to redeem that aspect of your life?

2. How can you discover more about your identity as a beloved daughter of God?

3. Is there a part of your story where you are enslaved to sin? How does the Church, like a mother, desire your freedom and joy?

Questions for Conversation

1. Christ does not promise us a life free from pain and suffering. But he knows what this suffering is like, and he promises victory. How can you witness to the victory of the Resurrection?

2. Are there certain teachings in the life of the Church that you wrestle with? What are ways that you can explore the truths of those teachings with other women in your life?

3. To love someone is to will their good. What are ways that you can grow in loving others in your daily life?

Come Holy Spirit, living in Mary. Reveal the light of Christ's face in my life. Help me to remember the suffering that Christ endured for my sake and the love that burns in his heart specifically for me as his beloved daughter. Form me more and more each day into the image of Christ, who held nothing back out of love for me. Amen.

A Letter to the Woman Longing to Belong

"Remember who you are and whose you are."
—Sister Thea Bowman

In 1979, Pope John Paul II returned to his home country of Poland for the first time since he'd been elected to the papacy. During those nine days in June, he reminded over six million Polish people about their true identity. "You are not who 'they' say you are," he said over and over again. "Let me remind you who you really are." He reminded them that they mattered. They belonged. They were good. They were created by a good God who loved them.

Today, more than forty years later, that message still echoes true. We need to be reminded again who we really are, who God says we are as his beloved daughters. We need reassurance that we matter and that we have a place. Far too often, we believe lies about our identity, and those lies leave us wondering if we have a place, if we truly belong.

Lizzy is a woman who champions the belonging and goodness of all those she comes in contact with. Through her joyful witness and contagious laughter, she reminds me daily that all of our unique talents and beautiful differences bring God glory.

71

If you need to be reminded that you are not who 'they' say you are, sister, this letter is for you.

Dear Sister,

How lovely are you? You, in all your differences, in every way you stand out from the others. No one's stature, heavenly fragrance, or life in the garden is just like yours. You have been assigned a great duty to bravely show the world that womanhood does not come in a box. In a world that is constantly spewing lies at us, we must boldly and proudly proclaim that our femininity is not found through what we do but who we are.

If you're anything like me, this isn't an easy call to live out. As a little girl, I struggled to feel a sense of belonging. Having been born with a disability that affects the way I walk shaped my social experience in a way that permanently altered the way I receive love. Growing up with spina bifida gave me a perspective on uniqueness that I do not think I could have attained any other way, and I will always count that a blessing.

At age two, I felt unstoppable. I had a loving home and everything I needed. One day, while playing at the park across the street, I learned that I evidently didn't have everything I needed, that according to others, something was wrong with me. Another little girl came over to me, pointed at my leg braces, and said, "WHAT are those?! Those are so ugly." Shame immediately cast down on me. On this day, I accepted that my disability was a shameful thing to be kept under the radar. My tiny, extroverted self suddenly wanted to hide. And so I did, for as long as I could stand being alone. It wasn't being different that scared me, it was feeling like an outcast.

As I got older, my legs got stronger every day and so did I. I learned more about my spina bifida and the uniqueness of my body. At age thirteen, I thought to myself one day, "No one is exactly like me," and for the first time, I didn't completely hate that.

I wrestled with the "whys" of life until I finally started allowing Christ to show me the beauty of my uniqueness. Every flower in his garden is called to a different path. I will never be a rose because he made me to be a wildflower.

Perhaps you were bullied as a child and are still battling a bad self-image. Maybe you were told as a little girl that you would never be beautiful. Perhaps you, too, have a health condition that caused you to feel like a misfit. Maybe you've battled an eating disorder or mental illness that has drained you of any knowledge of your beauty. Maybe you're facing a life-altering breakup and you feel that you have nothing left to offer the world.

These burdens, as painful as they are, unite us in our womanhood, because most of us know what it's like to suffer through growth. Despite that, we are all different flowers, we all belong to the same garden, and it wouldn't have its radiance without you.

Do not be afraid to be the flower that God has called you to be. Surround yourself with godly women, but remember you are not supposed to become just like them. Instead, look to Our Lady as your example of a woman who followed God's will in unwavering trust. Her faith did not rely on the opinions of others because her eyes were set on the One who made her for that life-giving purpose.

When this world decides we are no longer useful to it, it will turn us away. This is where the radical teachings of Christ come into play as he says, "My Kingdom is not of this world." My dear friend, you will never flourish in places you were not meant to be. Give yourself permission to be freed from another woman's calling; it was made for her, and you alone were made for yours. Never forget that you are a unique person too. Rest in the hope of his garden. There you can love courageously, live abundantly, and bloom gloriously.

Lizzy

Lizzy Grace Dowd is a twenty-one-year-old daughter, sister, friend, writer, traveler, spina bifida advocate, curly redhead, and professional goofball. She strives to cultivate a brighter, more compassionate world where every flower crafted by God knows their place in his garden. She resides in central Iowa, where she is working towards a career in music therapy. When she's not tweeting, you can find her thrift shopping, singing in the sunlight, or dancing like a fool in the grocery store.

Questions for Reflection

1. Do you believe that your differences, unique talents, gifts, and personality make you lovely?
2. Have you been tempted to define your worth as a woman not in who you are but by what you do?
3. Where is God calling you to flourish?

Questions for Conversation

1. What are some lies from the world about what it means to be a woman that you have believed, and how does God desire to speak truth into these lies?
2. When have you suffered through growth? How have crosses you've carried in your life helped you discover more of the woman God has created you to be?
3. Have you ever tried to fit yourself into a box, to look exactly like someone else instead of who you are? How is the Lord inviting you to step into your own unique call?

Come Holy Spirit, living in Mary. When the world tells me to hide in shame, to believe that my unique differences make me unsightly, reassure me of the beautiful and intentional way that I have been created. Help me to hear the specific and distinct call that you have placed in my heart, and to bloom exactly in the way you desire for my life. Amen.

A Letter to the Woman Looking for Healthy Friendships

*"In this house, all must be friends, all must be loved,
all must be held dear, all must be helped."*
—St. Teresa of Avila

When I first moved to a new city after getting married, I realized that making friends as an adult was more challenging than I expected.

It felt like I was back in kindergarten again, trying to make connections and form friendships. But I wasn't able to become instant friends with other girls just because we wore the same shoes and played the same games on the playground. In fact, I didn't even know where to begin. So when I reached out to the few friends that I knew in the area about how to get involved in this brand new city while living a brand new vocation, they told me I needed to get in touch with Kelly.

Kelly is a woman who is a champion of authentic friendship. She not only has a passion for being an authentic friend to the women in her life but also equips other women to do the same through her involvement with women's ministry.

Years after that move, I am blessed to call Kelly a dear friend of mine, and I've been honored to witness her mission to help all women that she encounters experience healthy friendship.

If you're longing for healthy friendship with the women in your life, sister, this letter is for you.

Dear sister,

Okay, I'll say it: authentic, feminine friendships are hard. They require time. Trust me, I know, there is not enough time in a day. Friendships uncover the wounds in the depths of our hearts that haven't been healed. I don't want to go there. There's vulnerability, the uncomfortableness of being truly seen, emotionally naked. I definitely don't want to go there. Then, there are risks of being judged and unloved. No thank you. Comparison overflows and then all of a sudden, we're not good enough.

But dear sister, we fall short of the charity Christ calls us to if we continue in this state of mind.

If we go to our beloved Father, give him our time, show him our brokenness, and give him our hearts, he will show us our worth. He will confirm and reaffirm, a million times if needed, our identity as his daughters. He will see the depths of our hearts and say to us, "You are enough just as you are. You are known and loved by me."

Let him speak this truth in our hearts, healing the wounds of our brokenness. Let him overflow into our daily lives, into our surface level friendships. Because just as he transforms our hearts, he will transform these friendships into authentic ones.

We can learn so much about authentic, feminine friendships from Mary and St. Elizabeth in the Visitation (see Lk 1:39–56). In this encounter, Mary and Elizabeth see each other the way God sees them. Elizabeth isn't overcome with envy or comparison when she sees Mary, but she says, "Blessed are you among women, and blessed is the fruit of your womb" (Lk 1:42). Dear sisters, we must ask the Lord to remove the layers of comparison, jealousy, envy, and insecurities that have overtaken our hearts and eyes. We have to ask him for hearts and eyes that see how he sees and love how he loves.

This is hard stuff, I know. I most certainly fall short of seeing sisters in Christ the way the Lord sees them. Comparison and envy creep in and intertwined are the lies from the devil. Praise the Lord for the Holy Spirit. Just as Elizabeth was filled with the Holy Spirit (see Lk 1:41), may we also call on the Holy Spirit in these times.

With the Holy Spirit, we can also learn not only to receive the gift of each other but also to offer the gift of our very selves in an authentic, feminine friendship. Mary offers her very (pregnant) self to Elizabeth as she travels in haste to see her (see Lk 1:39–40). Elizabeth receives her as a gift, with the lens of God, and humbly responds, "And why is this granted me, that the mother of my Lord should come to me? For behold, when the voice of your greeting came to my ears, the babe in my womb leaped for joy" (Lk 1:43–44).

In response, Mary again offers herself to Elizabeth and expresses vulnerability in her canticle (Lk 1:46–55).

Dear sisters, let us not always seek for what we can get out of a friendship, but let us offer our very selves in humility and vulnerability. Let's greet each other with the same joy. After all, the Visitation is the second joyful mystery! We can encourage one another in the different ways each of us have said yes to God's plan. In authentic friendship with other women, we can celebrate the gift that we each are and not be consumed by what we are going to get out of a friendship.

Mary and Elizabeth show us so many things about an authentic, feminine friendship, but perhaps the most important would be that authentic, feminine friendships should point us to Christ and glorify him.

We're never going to be perfect at these friendships. Instead, we can strive for a friendship like Mary and Elizabeth. By the grace of God, these friendships are obtainable. But we need to pray for the grace for this kind of friendship. So if you're struggling with this kind of beautiful and authentic friendship with women in your life, befriend Mary and Elizabeth. They can help us, so let's begin by spending time praying with the Visitation. Let them bring us to the Sacred Heart of Jesus.

Mary and Elizabeth, pray for us!

In Christ through Mary,

Kelly

Kelly Maghe is a full-time working wife and mommy in Kansas City. You can find her and her husband taking walks in the park or hammocking under the trees on a nice sunny day. When she is not working, she is building relationships with women and plugging them into

Kansas City's Catholic Young Adult Women's Ministry, Sisterhood. She finds joy in hosting dinner parties and the life and food shared at the dinner table. Her creative outlet is her blog, where she shares a little bit of style, a little bit of life, and a whole lot of faith. You can find her at kellypnugent.com.

Questions for Reflection

1. Have you looked for self-worth in the friendships in your life? Can you turn to Christ in prayer and ask him to tell you who he says you are?
2. Is the Lord inviting you to grow deeper in your friendship with women in your life? How can you encounter them in your daily life?
3. What are some of the wounds in your heart that you've experienced in your friendships with women? How does Christ want to heal those wounds so that you can grow in authentic friendship with women in your life?

Questions for Conversation

1. Have you been blessed in friendship with women who have shown you the Sacred Heart of Jesus? How have they led you to Christ during your time in friendship with them?
2. Is there a particular part of Mary's visit with St. Elizabeth that strikes you? What are some things that Mary and Elizabeth's relationship can teach you about friendship?

3. What are ways that we can strive with grace to overcome comparison and jealousy in our friendships with other women?

Come Holy Spirit, living in Mary. Inspire me to receive and give the gift of friendship with other women in my life. Help me strive for the humility and authenticity that I witness in your friendship with St. Elizabeth. Transform my friendships with women to be friendships that glorify you and reveal you to this world. Amen.

A Letter to the Woman Who Doesn't Think She's Creative

"Not all are called to be artists in the specific sense of the term. Yet . . . all men and women are entrusted with the task of crafting their own life: in a certain sense, they are to make of it a work of art, a masterpiece."
—Pope St. John Paul II

As you may be able to tell from the title of this book, John Paul II's "Letter to Women" that he penned in 1995 is one of my favorite things that he wrote during his papacy. But he also wrote another letter called the "Letter to Artists." In this letter, he encourages all of us to make our lives a creative masterpiece, a work of art.

For many of us, this idea of being an artist and experiencing and interacting with creativity can cause us to squirm. Some of us struggle to see ourselves as creative, and there's a lot of shame around this idea of creativity in today's world. Maybe you were told to focus on something that pays the bills. Or maybe someone told you that you weren't creative enough. But the truth is that we have to be able to experience creativity in some shape or form in our lives. We can't just consume creative works. We have to contribute to the beauty found in today's world.

Anna is a woman who has inspired me with her passion and creativity. Her attention to detail and the way she pours her heart into her handcraft regularly inspires me to pursue creativity in my own life.

If you have a desire to create but don't think you can possibly attempt anything creative, sister, this letter is for you.

Dear sister,

Creativity is this intriguing, sometimes frustrating, and ultimately incredibly rewarding dance. There is such a beautiful tension about creativity because it is both a gift and a skill. It is both within and outside of your control. These both/ands are really important to remember!

I create things for a living, and I absolutely love it. But that doesn't mean the process is always smooth. Sometimes a new product or design will come together in a heartbeat, but other times, most times even, it takes months and months and trial after trial before things click. And sometimes things never do. Not every idea you have is going to work! But just because there is a struggle doesn't mean I'm not creative, and if you struggle creatively, that doesn't mean you're not creative, either. The truth is that sometimes struggle is part of the process. And if I've learned anything about creativity, it's that you have to trust the process. If there's something in you that wants to make something, keep showing up.

So often we get caught up in what we think the end result is supposed to be or in comparing our ideas and our efforts to someone else's. Perhaps you can think of a time you felt insecure because of someone else's creativeness. Believe me, I get it! Women know, deep down, that we are created to be creative. After all, the truth that God has given women the immense privilege and responsibility to create is written into our very bodies and on our hearts. So when we feel as though we're not creative, it can hurt to see others who are.

If we are honest with ourselves, though, I think that many times when we feel we're not creative (or smart, or funny, or pretty, etc.), what we're really telling ourselves is that we're not creative *enough*—we're not creative compared to someone else. And then we feel we are not good enough, period.

Comparison like that can be crippling, and it's something we have to fight against. If what you want is to be creative, then just do it: make something! You may get it right on the first try or you may have to come at it dozens of different ways, but as G. K. Chesterton said, if something is worth doing, it is worth doing badly. Try and don't be afraid to try again. And don't be afraid to take a break and come back to it later on.

Creativity isn't magic; it involves skill, and skill comes from practice. If you stretch and flex those creative muscles, "being creative" can become easier. There's discipline involved in creativity, and that discipline to dig deeper and go again is what helps you break through the creative blocks.

But on the other hand, creativity isn't something we simply control, or are owed, or get to demand. Creativity is also a gift, and for it to bear fruit, we must recognize and receive this gift. From the first moment of our existence, everything we are and have is a gift from God. And he is so loving and so generous that he enables us to share in his creative work, and as women, we get to do this in a unique way.

Receiving a gift should always entail wonder, both at the goodness of the gift itself and at the generosity of the giver, which itself is also a gift. True creativity requires wonder, and vulnerability, and humility; it needs an open heart ready to receive the goodness of creation and of God's love, and then to offer it back.

Mary's fiat is really creativity par excellence. Because she was first and foremost trusting in and open to God's love and will for her, she was able to be vulnerable and place her future in his hands. And what wonders he worked through and with her!

That is where we all have to begin, and where we have to return to again and again, trusting that creating is worth saying yes to. And then, show up.

Hearts up,

A n n a

Anna Camacho is the owner and maker of CORDA. Her hand-crafted products bridge the sacred and the secular, bringing the faith into everyday moments, and feature fragrances inspired by saints and the Catholic faith. Born and raised in the Midwest, she loves being surrounded by family and big, open skies. Learn more at www.cordacandles.com.

Questions for Reflection

1. Would you describe yourself as creative? If not, what are some ways that you can foster wonder in your life

and be inspired by the goodness of God as a creative creator?

2. Have you been so caught up in the end result of a creative endeavor that you're unable to exist and enjoy the process of creating? What are some ways that you can be present in the process of creativity?

3. How can you recognize the gift of creativity and receive it in your own life? Where is God desiring you to create and bear fruit?

Questions for Conversation

1. What are some ways that you enjoy stretching your creative muscles?

2. Have you been tempted to compare your creativity to someone else's gifts and talents? What are some ways that you can appreciate the gifts of others and the gifts and talents Christ has given you too?

3. What can Our Lady and her fiat teach us about creativity?

Come Holy Spirit, living in Mary. You've blessed me with unique ways to participate in your creativity. Today I ask that you free me from the things holding me back from rejoicing and playing in this creativity as a woman fully alive in you. Inspire me to return to this creative process again and again, and equip me to make my very life a masterpiece in your love. Amen.

$\mathcal{A}$ Letter to the Woman Longing for Freedom

"When suddenly you seem to lose all you thought you had gained, do not despair. You must expect setbacks and regressions. Don't say to yourself 'All is lost. I have to start all over again.' This is not true. What you have gained you have gained. . . . When you return to the road, you return to the place where you left it, not to where you started."
—Henri J. M. Nouwen, *The Inner Voice of Love*

Do you long for freedom in your life? Is your heart and soul exhausted from wrestling against sin and shame?

I remember, when I was in college, sitting in confession with our campus chaplain and crying. I was struggling with major sins in my life, and it felt like I wasn't making much progress in becoming the woman God created me to be.

I remember distinctly saying, "I'm struggling. I don't have it together. But everyone thinks I'm fine, that I'm okay, and that I have it all together. I don't want them to know that I'm struggling. Would anyone want to be friends with me, to be in conversation with me, if they knew what I was going through?"

It's easy to believe the lies from the devil that are haunting our hearts as women. The lies that we are too much or not enough. The lies that everyone sees our brokenness and doesn't care or that people would run away if they knew the pain in our heart. But Christ sings truth over our stories. He invites us to freedom.

Erica's vulnerability and honesty is a light for those who are struggling to overcome the darkness of addiction and shame. She speaks with clarity and wisdom about her addiction to alcohol and the ways God has transformed her story into one of freedom and healing.

If you're living in the throes of any kind of addiction and battling secrecy, sister, this letter is for you.

Dear sister,

I had no hope back then. All my attempts to crawl out of the deep hole I was living in were futile.

I was twenty-five and living in Brooklyn. I had graduated with honors from an amazing university, I served as a missionary in Brazil for eighteen months, and was making life in a big city. But in the secrecy of my heart, I was only holding on by a string. I had started drinking in college and it quickly got out of my control.

I thought I could solve the issue by learning how to love better in serving others. Unfortunately, when I returned to the States after volunteering, I still didn't know how to cope as a young American girl. I drank to feel okay in my skin, to relate to other people my age, to have fun, to escape, to mask my depression. I blamed everything else for my misery: a job I didn't love, being unlovable and unable to keep a steady boyfriend, stress of finances, etc. What I didn't see was how much the drinking was actually preceding much of the despair.

When my spiritual director pointed out that I might have an addiction to alcohol, I told him that I did not and I did not know how I would be able to live without it. I was certain if I didn't drink anymore, I wouldn't have any friends, I would never be able to date, and I would no longer have any fun. I was unable and unwilling to look at this part of my life that I had no control over.

For health reasons, I decided I wouldn't drink for a month. I thought it was a matter of will and that I could just stop. I managed to not drink for an entire week before I gave into the physical and mental craving. Then after drinking too much the night before, I would say the next day that I wasn't going to drink that night, only to find myself having too many drinks out with friends. It was out of my control. It didn't matter how certain I was that I would have only one beer; after one, there was always another and another.

However, since I seemed to only binge a few nights a week, I thought I was like everyone else my age. I thought it was normal. The difference became apparent though when my desire and intention was to not drink on any given night and then waking up the next morning hungover and ashamed. There was no freedom. This dependence brought me no joy, added despair to my life, and I couldn't stop.

The day that I finally admitted to myself that I actually did have a problem was just like all the others. There wasn't something catastrophic that happened, my life wasn't in shambles, and there is nothing that I can point to other than a moment of grace. Grace entered in and a sliver of light beckoned me out of the darkness. I recall that there was a sigh of relief as I realized I could get help.

It was so scary to walk into that first Alcoholics Anonymous group. It was scary to first admit to strangers that I was an alcoholic. But sitting in a room hearing other people's stories, some similar to mine and some not, I felt a sense of kinship and belonging. If they could do it, then maybe there was hope for me.

I no longer had to hide in the darkness—live two separate lives—and I could begin to address the shame that I was drowning in. My favorite teaching in our Christian faith is the idea that darkness cannot overcome the Light. In the Light, there is healing and freedom.

At first, I thought the issue was just a matter of drinking and not drinking. What I discovered was that it wasn't really about the drinking at all. It was a spiritual malady. I was using alcohol to cope with and escape from life, and now without alcohol, I had a lot of inner healing that needed to happen.

I couldn't find freedom from my addiction alone. It is only with and through others that I could begin to recover from alcoholism, not merely abstain from drinking. It was like I was living in a dark, dark closet with a lot of spider webs. To let the light in and begin the work, I had to fling the door open and let the light enter in. And once that light flooded in, it revealed a room full of cobwebs that needed to be cleared.

Nothing happened overnight. I had to learn to be vulnerable and really let other people into my life. I had to allow for a spiritual transformation to take place and to sit in a lot of uncomfortable feelings that I had spent much of my life running from. My faith journey could no longer be about a transactional relationship with God where I got what I wanted in return for following the rules. I had to instead admit my powerlessness, allow God to work and move in my life and keep showing up to what was in front of me. And that is where I found freedom.

Recovery is not something that happens once, but an ongoing practice. There are, like anything else, ebbs and flows. It is not magic. But there are tools that I learned for a new way of living. Tools like prayer and meditation, calling another person to ask for advice, reaching my hand out to someone in need, asking for forgiveness, righting my wrongs, and going to meetings. Even still, six years later, I sometimes choose not to pick up those tools. In those times, while I am not bound by drinking alcohol, I am certainly not living joyously and freely. Then, in hearing another's story, in hearing that I'm not alone, I am reminded what's there for me to return to.

To you, living in the hidden secrecy of shame, you who fears both to be found out and also to continue on the road you're on, there is hope! Hope is not lost! There are others who have walked before you, and you do not have to face the journey alone. Light shines in the darkness and darkness will not overcome it.

Christ, be our light.

Erica

Erica Tighe Campbell is the founder of Be A Heart, a company that designs and sells modern Catholic goods. She lives with her husband, Paul, and their daughter, Frances, in San Antonio, Texas. She graduated from DePaul University in Chicago with a Bachelor of Arts in sociology. She served as a volunteer with Heart's Home in Salvador, Brazil for eighteen months. She is originally from Phoenix and lived in Brooklyn and Los Angeles. She believes in the cycle of life, death, and resurrection in our everyday lives and seeks to give hope to the hopeless. You can find her at www.beaheart.com.

Questions for Reflection

1. Have you found yourself using a substance to escape from something in your life?
2. Are you wrestling with an addiction? Are you ready to admit your powerlessness and allow God into this part of your heart?
3. Do you know someone who you can turn to in healthy vulnerability and trust with this part of your story?

Questions for Conversation

1. What kinds of addictions have we come to believe are normal in today's culture? How can we begin to bring these addictions to the light of God's truth?
2. Recovery ebbs and flows. What are ways that you can find hope when things seem to be going backward in the healing process?
3. One lie that the devil tries to tell us when we're battling addiction is that we're totally alone. But if you're seeking healing and freedom, you're not alone—people have walked this path before you. Who is some-

one in your life who, with grace and virtue, has found freedom in God?

Come Holy Spirit, living in Mary. Shine a light through the darkness of the addiction I am wrestling with, the lies of secrecy and shame, and the feelings of despair. Bring your joy and your freedom, your healing and your strength. Never permit me to believe that I can (or should) overcome this darkness on my own. Be a safe shelter for me, and bring me into your glorious light. Amen.

A Letter to the Woman Who's Healing

"Be certain that if you stand beneath the Cross you will never be lost. The Devil has no power over those souls who weep near the Cross. My daughter, how many would have abandoned me, if I had not crucified them. The Cross is a very precious gift, and many virtues can be learned through it."
—Jesus to St. Gemma Galgani

The cross of Christ makes sense of suffering, and Christ knows the depths of our suffering like no one else. He walked before us, enduring a horrific passion and death. He suffered first, then turns back to those of us here on earth and invites us to suffer for and with him. God doesn't ask us to heal our own wounds or to ignore them. Instead, the Lord offers us a chance to unite our wounds to the wounds of Christ.

Just what does it look like to unite our pain to the heart of Jesus? Mary Lenaburg is a woman who knows the realities of loss and suffering. But she also is one of the most amazing witnesses I know to both the sorrow and beauty that comes with healing. Through her writings and wisdom, I have learned that we can encounter God even in our deepest wounds—and it is in those wounds that God desires to redeem our story and bring glory to his name.

If your heart is aching from wounds and you're longing for Christ's healing in your story, sister, this letter is for you.

Dear sister,

I sit in the same pew that I did every Sunday she was alive. I look upon the altar and nothing feels right. My heart is heavy with grief and my mind whirls with questions I know will never be answered this side of heaven. I'm tired of hurting and weary of grief. I just can't do it anymore. I cannot carry this weight in my heart. I want my daughter back, but I know that is not to be. So I sit there staring at the tabernacle not knowing if I have the energy to believe that God really is a God of mercy and healing. At that moment, it doesn't feel like it at all.

I know I need to change the narrative in my head. I'm allowing doubt to take hold, and the voice that whispers lies is getting louder. I get up and get in the confession line. Maybe a little soul cleaning will help. I wait. I wonder if I will ever feel normal again, if I will ever be able to be in this sacred space and not think of my dead daughter whom I loved with all I had. The light turns green above the door and it's my turn to enter in. I sit, make the sign of the cross, and begin. After just one sin confessed, Father stops me and begins to ask questions, probing my heart, digging a little deeper to get to the root. I'm annoyed. I just want to be done. He knows it and is trying to be a good father. He patiently waits for my answer saying, "Mary, God cannot heal what you do not give him. Remember that he will never ask you to do more than he has done for you."

I break.

Tears come and words spill out of my mouth straight from the depths of my heart. "I want her back. Why did God have to take her? I'm mad. I'm tired of carrying this pain. I just want to be able to remember the joy and leave the pain behind."

He smiles and simply says, "Healing is painful, Mary. When you have loved so well, the wound is deep and takes a long time to scab over. Then it itches and irritates, and finally, when it's healed, there is still a weak point in the skin that's tender. That's the way your heart will always be when it comes to Courtney. Tender. Sensitive to the pain of her loss. That's just how life goes. Sadness and joy, walking hand in hand."

I tell him I am not a fan and he chuckles. "No one is." Then I finish my confession, pouring out what I have kept hidden for so long. There is freedom in sharing from the darkest places in my soul. I feel lighter and more at peace. Maybe I truly can allow God to heal where I am broken. I ponder this for a moment, then Father gives me my penance.

"Go pray an Our Father, nice and slow, thinking about every word. Remember how you used to pray it with Courtney. Invite her into that prayer and let God begin the healing of your heart. We pray and I go back to that pew, tears still coming, remembering every Mass my girl and I attended. I could hear her favorite songs sung by the choir. I chuckled at the thought of a certain priest preaching and how she would hum louder the longer he went on.

I began to pray the Our Father as I had been instructed, and I knew my Courtney was right there with me. I took it line by line asking God into each and every corner of my grief filled and hardened heart. I imagined a warm light shining from the inside out. I asked for healing and perseverance and strength.

He heard me and answered my prayer.

Day by day, I began to feel lighter as the weariness slowly slipped away. I see the joy once more as the grief becomes part of my story but not what defines me. To lose a child is to lose the best part of yourself. I had been hemorrhaging out on the battlefield of life, and I knew I could fight no more unless the Divine Healer took over. That day, I opened the door and allowed him in. We now walk together through the pain and grief, resting in peace more often than I ever thought possible. There is tenderness where the wound was deepest.

This journey will take the rest of my life. Every time I begin to be swallowed up once more by the memories of what once was, he gently asks me to surrender it to him, for he has already healed it on the cross. Healing takes time, my friends. It's not an instant thing; it's a process of letting go and allowing God into the hard places where the wounds are so deep that you aren't sure if it's even possible to heal. But all things are possible with God.

Blessings,

Mary

Mary Lenaburg is a highly sought-after international public speaker and evangelizer with a strong background in women's and youth ministry. She is known for her engaging speaking style which incorporates personal storytelling, layered with deep emotion and humor to assist in communication of the theme of the talk.

Her bestselling book Be Brave in the Scared *is an uplifting account of human frailty (and stubbornness) surrendered to faith. Lenaburg tells the heart-rending story of how caring for her severely disabled daughter affected her self-image, marriage, family life, and faith.*

Although she initially struggled to accept God's will and her own limitations, Lenaburg ultimately learned how to trust God. She found in that trust inexplicable joy, even during the most difficult days of her life. She writes boldly and authentically about challenges we all encounter, such as trials with control, blame, exhaustion, fear, and acceptance.

Mary and her husband have been happily married for thirty-one years, finding joy among the ashes after having lost their disabled daughter Courtney in 2014. They live in Northern Virginia with their grown son Jonathan.

Mary continues to embrace her father's advice: "Never quit, never give up, never lose your faith. It's the one reason you walk this earth. For God chose this time and place just for you, so make the most of it."

Questions for Reflection

1. Are there wounds in your heart that are so deep that you wonder if you could ever find healing? Do you believe that this healing is possible with God?

2. When was the last time that you encountered Christ and the healing sacramental grace of Penance? Is the Lord inviting you back to this sacrament, and if so, how will you respond to his invitation?

3. In moments of grief, how can you open the door of your heart and allow Christ's light to flood in?

Questions for Conversation

1. Where in your story have you experienced the reality that sadness and joy walk hand in hand?
2. Healing takes time. It doesn't happen in an instant. What are some ways that Christ has brought healing into your life?
3. How can we, as women, accompany each other better when we experience seasons of deep healing in our lives?

Come Holy Spirit, living in Mary. Come, divine physician. Today, I invite you into every part of my broken heart, even the parts that I've previously hidden from you out of shame or fear that there is too much here for your hand to heal. Bring comfort and rest to my weary soul, and reassure my tired heart that I am not alone in this journey, that you walk beside me every step of the way. Amen.

A Letter to the Woman Struggling with Comparison

"Yes, there is that voice, the voice that speaks from above and from within and that whispers softly or declares loudly: 'You are my Beloved, on you my favor rests.' It certainly is not easy to hear that voice in a world filled with voices that shout: You are no good, you are ugly; you are worthless; you are despicable, you are nobody—unless you can demonstrate the opposite."
—Henri J. M. Nouwen, *Life of the Beloved*

If you struggle and find yourself comparing your story to someone else's story, you're not alone. On bad days, it only takes me a few scrolls through Instagram before I sink into comparing my body, wardrobe, happiness, and holiness to the lives of the women in my feed. I'm going to take a safe bet and guess that you know what that struggle is like, since you turned to this letter.

We know we have a comparison problem. So how are we going to tackle it? It begins by realizing that our sister's success is not our failure. Your story will never be exactly like hers—thank goodness. If it was the same story, the world would miss out on the beauty that your life brings.

Beth is a woman whose honesty about her struggle against comparison has inspired me to tackle this battle head first in my own life. She isn't afraid to call out the truth that living a life of comparison and competition isn't healthy for us as Catholic women. But her example also shows me that the beauty of authentic friendship between women is totally possible.

If you've caught yourself comparing your body, your strengths, your weaknesses, your home, your family, or your life to women on Instagram, sister, this letter is for you.

Dear sister,

You dear, precious woman, you. Lean in and let me tell you a little story.

A few weeks ago, I stared at a picture of myself for several minutes, taking inventory of what I saw. White hair, saggy eyes, the beginnings of (heaven forbid) jowls. Some general puffiness, faint lines, but no real wrinkles to speak of. It almost felt like I was staring at a picture of somebody else. Someone who, granted, looked a lot like me, but just couldn't be me, could it? I mean, this is not what I see in the mirror and certainly not what I see in my mind's eye.

Ugh! I thought, physically shaking my head. *Here I go again. Comparing. Why do I do this to myself?*

See, I have a tendency to compare myself to, well, just about anyone and for any reason. I even compare myself to, well, myself. Try as I might, for me, comparison just isn't something I've been able to conquer. Far from it! Instead, it's something that I continue to work on both in prayer and in action each and every day.

But as I continue to stare at that photo, it seems that comparison is winning the battle.

I'm shocked by how white my hair looks in the sunlight. How is it that more than five years since my last dye-job, I still think of myself as someone with dark hair? I roll my eyes, look at my face again, then let my eyes move on down the topography of my person. There it is. Underarm flaps, a big soft belly, and cellulite. I see these things whenever I look in the mirror, but in my mind's eye, they just don't exist. Weird, right?

Has anything like this ever happened to you? I'm going to go out on a limb here and imagine that maybe it has. Like I said, though, I'm not the only one I compare myself to. I catch myself at it all the time.

Am I doing better or worse, working harder than or not as hard as that lady at the gym? Are my clothes more or less stylish than that woman's? Am I fatter or skinnier? Do I look older or younger?

And it certainly isn't just physical comparisons I make. Or can I say "we" now? I feel like maybe you're with me on this, so for the sake of generalizations, I'm going to switch over to "we." Cool? Cool.

We women tend to compare ourselves to others in all manner of imaginable ways. Her car is nicer than mine. Our children are better behaved than theirs. I can't have those people over for dinner because their house is so much nicer than ours. She can't possibly understand the stress I'm under as a working mom. She must think I've got all the time in the world for this since I stay home with my kids. I'm nowhere near as holy as that lady who goes to daily Mass. I'm so much holier than that non-church-goer.

Does any of that sound familiar? Yeah, I thought so.

Now, allow me to take you on a stroll down memory lane. Several years ago, my family and I took a trip to attend a wedding. The people who were getting married were very important to me and there would be many women there who I loved and hadn't seen in ages and ages. There were five of us in particular who'd grown up together. And this wedding would be the first time in a long time we would all be in one place.

Getting ready for the wedding, I fretted way more than I should have about my hair (that had gone gray while the others' hadn't) and the fact that my dress was tighter than it had been the last time I'd worn it (just a few months earlier). Surely, these other women were much happier with how they looked! I'd seen recent pictures of them on Facebook and thought they all looked amazing! I put more effort into my hair and makeup for this wedding and did more fussing at my children about their appearances and manners than I quite care to admit.

When we got to the wedding, sure enough, everyone looked wonderful! My kids were well-behaved and long-time family and friends were all thoroughly enjoying themselves. As the dancing kicked off, though, these ladies and I got to talking. In and among the reminiscences, the conversation naturally veered towards our jobs. One woman was an executive for a high-powered investment firm. One was a doctor who served on national committees in her field.

Another had recently become a nurse practitioner. There were women with doctorates and master's degrees.

And me? What was I doing with my life? Well, I was a mom. And a wife. I sang at church and volunteered with my kids' swim team. That was about it!

And as I said the words, I'm embarrassed to say that I felt myself growing smaller and smaller.

You see, friend, in comparing my professional accomplishments (or lack thereof) to theirs, I missed out on so much. Sure, it meant that I spent too much of the wedding reception in a funk rather than truly enjoying myself. But even more than that, I denied myself the joy I felt in my chosen vocation as a stay-at-home mom and the pride I felt in the amazing family my husband and I were raising. By comparing myself to them, it's like I was disregarding who God had made me to be and telling myself that he had somehow made them better. That is no way to think about yourself! When Theodore Roosevelt said that "comparison is the thief of joy," he wasn't wrong.

The more time we spend comparing ourselves to others (or heck, even to ourselves!), the less time we have to appreciate all that we've been given. When we spend too much energy fixating on the gifts of others, we subconsciously bury our own talents in the ground and totally forget to glorify the Lord with them.

So what I want you to take away from this letter, sister, is that comparison can't be the boss of you or me or any of us! Not anymore. Who's done more, done better, gotten farther? Who has more likes, comments, shares, followers? Who has the more important or "better" job? When we compare our accomplishments with those of other women, it's such a waste of time and energy!

I thank God that the older I get and the more I dive into my faith, comparison has less and less of a hold on me, creating the space for me to learn to love myself and let myself be loved by the One who created me. I pray that you, too, can do the same.

Beth

Beth Williby is a wife, mother, music minister, and writer. She and her husband of over twenty years have four children ranging in age from elementary school to college. She shares her thoughts on family, faith, and food on her blog, A Welcome Grace. *Beth is an enthusiastic proponent of good books, coffee with friends, and singing show tunes while cooking. Having grown up in the Midwest, she now calls Northeast Florida home.*

Questions for Reflection

1. When are you most likely to fall into the trap of comparison?
2. Have you felt underqualified, fraudulent, or "less-than" lately? What does God have to say about who you are?
3. How can you glorify God with your unique talents and gifts today?

Questions for Conversation

1. Have you struggled with comparison in your own life?

2. Why do we as women struggle with comparison, and
    how does Christ desire to heal us of this tendency to
    compare our bodies, our stories, and our lives to the
    women around us?

3. What is something that you can do today to combat
    the lies of comparison and worthlessness in your own
    life?

Come Holy Spirit, living in Mary. Give me the grace I need in this battle against comparison. Help me be grateful for the gifts and talents that you've given me and realize that the gifts and talents other women have been blessed with do not make me less. Instead of believing the lie that I am not good enough, reassure me that I am loved and beloved and that the women who I compare myself to are also your daughters. Amen.

A Letter to the Woman Intimidated by the Idea of Hospitality

"Hospitality means primarily the creation of free space where the stranger can enter and become a friend instead of an enemy. Hospitality is not to change people, but to offer them space where change can take place. It is not to bring men and women over to our side, but to offer freedom not disturbed by dividing lines."
—Henri Nouwen, *Reaching Out*

Inviting people into your home can be challenging. There have been multiple times where I've wanted to invite people inside my home and into my life, but I've stopped. I thought my home was too small or too messy. It seemed like no matter how hard I tried, my home would never measure up to the standards of perfection I'd created for myself. The virtue of hospitality seemed intimidating and unattainable.

Then I met Jennie. In our time as friends, Jennie has taught me so much about the beauty of simple hospitality. I've stood in awe of the authentic, honest way that she invites friends and strangers alike into the four walls of her family's home. When I spend time at her home or in her company, I can simply exist, and that is a joy and gift that I will be forever grateful for. After being welcomed into her home with her joyful celebration of hospitality, I have a confidence I've never had to do the same for my friends and neighbors. Hospitality isn't impossible, but it starts by letting go of perfectionism.

If you long for community but are afraid your home or heart is too messy to host anyone, sister, this letter is for you.

Dear sister,

I grew up in a home filled with people. Our front door was constantly open and seldom locked, as friends filtered in and out, card games ensued on the kitchen table, and neighborhood kids played basketball on the driveway at all hours of the day or night. My mom made sure our home was a safe and joyful place for anyone to find an open ear, a sympathetic smile, or at the very least, some brownie bites and pizza rolls.

So it follows that the words "come on over" seem to tumble out of my mouth before I've had an opportunity to carve a toy and shoe-free path from the front door to the table. Often there are already a handful of visitors already sitting there. And even better, many come over uninvited and unannounced. Through my mother's model of receptivity and generosity, I've witnessed that being hospitable isn't something you do but who you are; it is an attitude of the heart. When our hearts are open to receive whomever might walk through the door (or God forbid, the garage) and whatever burden he or she might carry, our homes will be as well.

We recently read the Gospel story of the road to Emmaus with our kids while our doors were closed and our lives on pause due to the coronavirus. I've heard the story countless times: two disciples traveling along the road, hearts heavy with sadness and rumor and confusion, when an unrecognizable visitor walks alongside them. They recount the story of Christ's crucifixion and resurrection. The visitor rebukes them for their slowness of heart and interprets to them the Scriptures. The disciples are inspired to invite the visitor into their homes, and it is there, in the breaking of the bread, where they see Jesus. But this time while reading the Gospel, it occurred to me that if these two disciples had not extended the invitation, Scripture tells us, Jesus would have continued on further. It is because of their act of hospitality that they were able to encounter Jesus. If they had withheld the invitation out of embarrassment at the state of their home, or out of concern that they had no food or drink or even if they had withheld the invitation out of fear of opening their hearts, they would have missed a great gift.

Jesus is counting on our receptivity and generosity to build his kingdom. He needs us to live out this key message of the Gospel and essential element of evangelization. After all, he sends his apostles out on mission two by two to enter into the homes and hearts of those willing to open themselves and hear his message. The whole kingdom of heaven is described as a giant party where all are welcome and fulfilled by God in his super-abundance! And most importantly, when we are animated by charity to open our homes and hearts, it is Christ we receive as a guest.

But here's the thing: the enemy is counting on this too. So when our culture hijacks this good and twists and contorts hospitality into industry only for professionals, when it becomes something unattainable that requires a clean house, a tight guest list and goat cheese, it is easy to feel overwhelmed and unworthy. In a world that prizes performance and perfection, it is easy to forget we are favored daughters of a God who loves us for our presence. It is easy to close our doors and our hearts and let Jesus travel on down the road.

And so this is how we must live this Gospel virtue: simply, poorly, and with great humility. We must live it with Cheez-Its and mediocre wine. It isn't necessary to have a signature cocktail and a charcuterie board; authentic hospitality requires only humility and toilet paper. I surrender my imperfect home and let it be a sign of my imperfect heart, letting it be open and messy as an act of solidarity with my guests who might also have a pile of toddler underwear near the toilet and a need for confession. I concede my calendar, which already feels too tight and too full, knowing hospitality is tied to availability. Our guests have hung garage shelving, joined a jam session, and helped pull science projects over the finish line because we have invited them into our sloppy lives with joy and gratitude.

The next time a neighbor lingers on your driveway, reject the lie that your home or your family doesn't measure up, and invite her in. In this humble act of hospitality, Christ is already working in us; let his grace fill in the gaps.

Love,

Jennie

Jennie Punswick is an instructor and missionary with the Holy Family School of Faith Institute. She is passionate about issues concerning discipleship, Catholic education, authentic Catholic family life, and the blessed chaos of young motherhood. She writes and speaks about these issues throughout the Archdiocese of Kansas City, Kansas. Jennie and her husband reside in Overland Park with their six children: Joseph, Lucia, Samuel, John, Catherine, and Cecilia.

Questions for Reflection

1. Are there women in your life who have welcomed you into their lives and their homes and shown you true hospitality? What have you learned about hospitality and authenticity from their witness in your life?
2. Is there someone in your life who the Lord is inviting you to reach out to in a spirit of hospitality? What are ways that you can create a place for them in your daily life?
3. Do you struggle with performance and perfectionism when it comes to hospitality? Today, can you ask the Lord to open the door of your heart so that you can welcome him into your heart and your life?

Questions for Conversation

1. What was your experience and understanding of hospitality when you were growing up?
2. Does hospitality make you nervous? What are some things that are standing in the way and keeping you from opening your life and home to others, and how does God desire to remove those obstacles so that you can encounter others and share his love with them?

3. What are some things in your life that you need to concede so that you can let go of the unattainable expectations of a hospitality industry and instead enter into simple, poor, and humble hospitality?

Come Holy Spirit, living in Mary. Accompany me as I examine my heart to discover what is holding me back from opening my heart and my home with authentic and humble vulnerability. As I open the door of my heart and the door of my home, grant me the grace to encounter each guest as Christ. Amen.

A Letter to the Woman in a Season of Discernment

"The best thing for us is not what we consider best, but what the Lord wants of us."
—St. Josephine Bakhita

Have you found yourself asking God (pleading with God!) to just tell you what he desires for your life? Maybe you're in a season of vocational discernment. Perhaps you're discerning things like where to live, what job to pursue, or the answer to a life changing decision you have to make. Discernment isn't easy. I've had many times in my life when I'm discerning and I just wish God would have written the answer out for me with an airplane in the sky or given me a literal sign.

But God speaks into the silence of our hearts, and he doesn't always say what we expect or want. Yet he asks us to trust him, to surrender our will to him, and to rest in the knowledge that he has a plan for our life.

If you're in a season of discernment, it's easy to feel alone as you navigate the process of discovering God's will and resigning yourself to his plan. But you're not alone. You're surrounded by women who know exactly what it's like to wonder if God is even aware of the desires of our heart or if we'll be forever in the dark to his will in our lives.

Nicole is a woman who speaks about the beauty and challenges of discernment so well, and I know her witness to the reality of discernment is bearing fruit in the lives of countless women.

If you're discerning where God is calling you, sister, this letter is for you.

Dear sister,

I thought my discernment journey would end with me lying prostrate in a habit, taking my vows with a beautiful, thriving religious community. Instead, it ended up with me face down on my bedroom floor, crying, unable to understand what just happened. Minutes prior, I had hung up the phone with Mother Superior, who informed me that after many visits to the monastery, countless conversations with the community, and endless encouragement from my spiritual director, my application for aspirancy with the community was rejected. I couldn't believe it. I was devastated. I was confused. And frankly, I was mad. Wasn't God supposed to give me the desires of my heart? I had already given up so much to follow him! What was I supposed to do now? Everything had pointed to this! The rejection was heavy, and I was never more confused about my purpose in life or unsure about my confidence in God than that afternoon in May 2018. However, after a year of grieving, I would come to make sense of my journey, realizing that sometimes we have to allow God to shift our desires to align with his.

Along my discernment journey, as my heart grew in desire to be a nun, I gave up significant opportunities like career advancements, romantic relationships, and living arrangements. I also gave up smaller luxuries like TV, vacations, and manicures to pursue what I believed the Lord wanted for me. I know many women say the thought of being called to a convent scares them. To me, it was the most thrilling possibility I could think of. I never feared being coulter-cultural, and this was about as counter-cultural as it could get. Perhaps this was where God would order my rebellious, autonomous heart. After all, life finally made sense after my conversion. And all I wanted to do was return everything to the One who gave me everything.

At the time, I thought I had figured it out. Religious life was a perfect fit for me, and I was enthusiastically willing to endure the sacrifices required to live the life. I had read over a dozen books on vocations and been on just about as many retreats. I was ready to cast the world off my shoulders to be a bride of Christ. While at the time, my aspiration seemed pure and full of zeal, looking back now, I can see I was harboring something that ran even deeper than my desire to live a radical life for Christ: the fear of living an ordinary life for Christ.

Had I become a sister, I would've made sacrifices that seemed difficult—maybe even impossible—to some people. Besides the obvious forgoing of a husband and children, people often wondered how I would go without things like a cell phone and sleeping in on Saturdays. But I felt much more prepared to give those things up than what I'd have to give up as a wife and mother: a markedly unique and distinctive life lived for the Lord.

After all, reciting Compline in the evenings seemed more significant than reading bedtime stories. Wearing a veil seemed more glamorous than donning a top knot. Waking up at five in the morning to pray seemed more distinctive than waking up at five to breastfeed. In short, I began to see that life as a nun would tempt me to pride in ways that being a lay woman wouldn't. Of course, this desire was comingled with pure and good intentions: wanting to serve God in a radical way, wanting to repent dramatically of my past sins, and wanting to fill my heart to its capacity with Jesus. And I know Christ saw this. I know he saw me striving with all my might to give my life for him. I thought I'd be able to give my most as a nun. God knew I'd give more of myself another way.

Do I feel two years of my life were wasted chasing a vocation to religious life? No! Scripture tells us that God wastes nothing of those who love him. "We know that in everything God works for good with those who love him, who are called according to his purpose" (Rom 8:28).

It may sound counterintuitive, but visiting with nuns and spending time on retreat with them showed me the qualities I want in my future marriage. Behind those walls, I saw the love St. Paul wrote about being lived out to the fullest. It was patient. It was kind. It did not envy or boast. It wasn't proud. It did not seek itself. It trusted, hoped, and persevered. God used my time of discernment to refine my heart and prepare me for the sacrificial love I'm called to give my future spouse.

So what would I say to any woman discerning her vocation? First, listen your desires! We're instructed to "take delight in the LORD and he will give you the desires of your heart" (Ps 37:4). Sometimes God will show us that our desires are a bit faulty, and that's OK! He will eventually reveal our deepest desires if we are earnestly seeking his will.

Secondly, take the plunge! We're also told, "Do not believe every spirit, but test the spirits to see whether they are of God" (1 Jn 4:1). Test out the desires of your heart. Go on dates. Attend discernment retreats. Put something into motion so God has something tangible to work with!

Thirdly, allow yourself to be surprised. "For my thoughts are not your thoughts, neither are your ways my ways" (Is 55:8–9). God sees us past, present, and future at all times. He knows what will make us happy and holy. Hold your assumptions loosely.

Finally, try and banish anxiety while you're navigating the unknown of your vocation. This can be the hardest part, but Jesus is with us every step of the way. "Be strong and of good courage; be not frightened, neither be dismayed; for the LORD your God is with you wherever you go" (Jo 1:9).

Know that whether God has planned for you to recite Compline, wear a habit, and rise early to pray or read bedtime stories, don a top knot, and breastfeed, each vocation glorifies God. Each vocation is extraordinary.

Blessings,

Nicole

Nicole is a school administrator living in the Bay Area, CA. After her conversion, she left the fashion industry to work in Catholic education. She also provides mentoring to young Catholic women in the areas of dating and discerning. You can find her on Instagram at @oheynicolehere. Her upcoming podcast Follow Your Fiat can be found on Instagram at @followyourfiat. When she's not working, she loves hiking, journaling, and all things baking.

Questions for Reflection

1. In this season of discernment, have you experienced anger, frustration, and confusion in the way that Christ is revealing his desire for your life? Have you expressed those feelings to God in prayer?
2. Have you put your discernment into motion? What are some tangible, actionable steps that you can take in your discernment that would help you discern God's will for you?
3. Do the unknown aspects of your discernment concern or frighten you? How is God desiring to strengthen you and give you courage in this season as you seek his will?

Questions for Conversation

1. Has your own discernment looked like what you expected it would? How has God surprised you in this season of discernment?
2. How is God refining your heart in this season of discernment? What have you learned about love as you've discerned his will in your life?

3. Is it difficult to hold your plans, desires, and assumptions loosely? What are ways that you can work to surrender to God and be receptive to your desires shifting according to God's will?

Come Holy Spirit, living in Mary. Align my desires and will to the good plans you have in store for me. In moments of confusion or frustration as I discern what your will and desire for my life are, help me remember that you are good and you work all things for good. Enter into my heart and surprise me with your grace and love. Amen.

A Letter to the Woman Struggling with Surrender

"To accept whatever He gives. And to give whatever it takes, with a big smile. This is the surrender to God. To accept to be cut to pieces and yet every piece to belong only to Him. This is the surrender. To accept all the people that come, the work that you happen to do. Today maybe you have a good meal and tomorrow maybe you have nothing. There is no water in the pump. Alright, to accept. And to give whatever it takes. It takes your good name, it takes your health, it takes . . . Yes, that is the Surrender. You are free then."

—St. Teresa of Calcutta

Does the word "surrender" bring comfort, or does it make you squirm? If you're like me (type A organizer over here), that word can be a hard pill to swallow. But Christ calls us to surrender everything, to hold nothing back, and to trust him completely.

But what about when he doesn't fulfill the desires of your heart—even the desires he placed in your heart? What about when trusting him is hard and you want to grasp onto your plans?

Ingrid is a woman who has inspired me with her radical surrender. In the years I've been blessed to know her and call her friend, I've watched her navigate confusing and uncertain situations. She's leaned into the hard and found solace in the hope that comes from a relationship with Christ. Ingrid has taught me to savor the little moments and to surrender situations of all sizes to the Lord and Divine Providence.

If the idea of surrendering it all to God leaves you more worried and upset than peaceful, sister, this letter is for you.

Dear sister,

I am scared of the dark. I am also scared of fish. I am particularly prone to letting fear and overwhelming situations get the best of me. I have cried and screamed and cussed out of frustration in scenarios where most people keep their cool. My family has said I'm "a bit dramatic." But there was one day where I had to forgo all of this and survive.

During my junior spring of college, I traveled to Tempe, Arizona to compete at Nationals with my university's club triathlon team. I had been relatively noncommittal in my triathlon career leading up to this race, so this would be the first time I ever did an open water swim. I grew up going to the lake, so I figured that would be enough experience, and I had done several mile-long swims to make sure I was capable of the distance. I was ready. The moment the air horn blew and our wave started, I stuck my head in the water and realized I was not ready. Not ready at all.

I couldn't see anything in the water. People were kicking and splashing on all sides, accidentally elbowing me as they swam past. I dog-paddled to an open area to get more space to begin my freestyle stroke but it made no difference. I couldn't shake the fact that I couldn't see beneath me. What if I swim away from the buoy? Are there any fish below me? Am I even moving? What if I get too tired? What if one of the safety pins holding my broken uniform together (a fun pre-race emergency) stabs me and I can't get my wetsuit off in the water and end up bleeding out in the middle of this lake?

Fear overcame my whole being. The adrenaline was not pushing me to do what I had trained for; it was spiraling me into a panic attack. The one piece of preparation that did come in handy was a survival book I had recently finished. Page after page declared the importance of rising above your emotions in a life-or-death situation and taking small, calculated actions aimed at your survival. Yes, there were several race officials in canoes around us in case of emergency, but there were also over fifty women in the water, and there is never a guarantee the officials see everything.

From my view, the moment was life-or-death: give into fear, panic, and drown, or surrender that fear, calm down, and live. I flipped onto my back so I could breathe freely and at least see the sky above me, counting out deep breaths with every backstroke. I watched a bridge pass above me and occasionally turned over to make sure I was still moving towards the turn buoy. All the while, I kept counting and breathing and reminding myself that being controlled by fear would not help me survive. Eventually, I felt relaxed enough to resume the freestyle stroke I had trained with, and I completed the race safely.

I speak often about the way that endurance sports are special to me because I find them deeply spiritual in nature. St. Peter alludes to this connection in his second letter to Timothy: "I have fought the good fight, I have finished the race, I have kept the faith" (2 Tm 4:7–8). Similarly, an excerpt from the Catechism speaks of taking up contemplative prayer in a way that sounds an awful lot like being on a training plan: "[Make] time for the Lord, with the firm determination not to give up, no matter what trials and dryness one may encounter" (CCC 2710). That day in the lake was a lesson in how necessary surrender is to our life, to our very breath. Surrender—acknowledging my fears and letting them go as I floated in the water—was the act that kept me alive.

When I began college, I took a grand leap into the unknown by accepting a scholarship for business school. Throughout my first two years, it became apparent that God was not calling me into the corporate world and that the path taking me to that university had a lot more to do with church, culture, and relationships than it did the actual degree I was receiving. I stuck it out in my major program but started looking for post-graduate opportunities to complete a year of service with a mission that better aligned with my gifts and passions.

As senior year approached, I felt God nudging me on a path I never expected. He wanted me to enter the mission field of Catholic education and become a teacher. Thus began a long process of applying, interviewing, praying, applying to more programs, waiting, interviewing, and waiting. There was so much waiting. Time was ticking away, and many of my classmates had secured jobs months ago. The further along I went, the more clouded I felt my path became. It was just like being in the lake again; I couldn't see a single thing that lay in front of me. Fear was gripping me. What if I didn't get a single offer? What if I got this whole path wrong?

I spoke these fears to God in prayer in the midst of my spring break trip to New Mexico. I was begging God for the grace to surrender within that uncertainty. The weeks were approaching when I would begin receiving acceptance decisions from the teaching programs I had applied to, and I had my sights set on one in particular. I took comfort in the fact that, while the future beyond my graduation date was a mystery, I still had my friends at school and an upcoming triathlon season to look forward to. This was March of 2020. Perhaps you can guess what happened next.

Less than an hour after I finished my prayer, feeling optimistic with the present consolations, the COVID-19 pandemic spurred the cancelation of the end of my senior year, caused the sudden conclusion of my triathlon season, and sent my college best friends back to their hometowns. Later that day, I found out I had been placed on the waitlist for the teaching program I so badly wanted. Suddenly, the fog shrouding my life path was so thick I couldn't even see my feet below me. I sobbed and grieved the sudden losses, so overcome by everything that I couldn't even feel my own fears. I had no choice but to surrender into the arms of the Father—who, mind you, felt distant and invisible in this time—and let him carry me along this path I could no longer traverse.

To surrender is not to say you aren't afraid or that you lack desires and doubts. Surrender is managing those fears and feelings by turning them over to God and refusing to let them dictate the course of your life. If I had continued to force control over my situation, I might not have heard the Lord gently guiding me along the path he carefully paved for me because it didn't move in the direction I expected. Yet he knew (far better than I did) what was best for me, and in surrender, I was able to receive that gift. My good sister, it's okay to feel afraid. We all do. But life—spiritually and physically—is not found when we let fear overwhelm us. Life lies on the other side of surrender.

Ingrid

Someday, Ingrid Herrenbruck would like to be canonized the patron saint of Birkenstocks. She was proudly raised in the great state of Kansas, but now resides in St. Louis, Missouri where she teaches fifth grade at a Catholic school. Outside of the classroom, she can be found riding her bike, playing Debussy on the piano, or drinking specialty coffee from her corgi mug. The girls she'd pick for her epic Catholic basketball team are Dorothy Day, St. Teresa of Avila, St. Edith Stein, and St. Katharine Drexel (and Our Lady of Guadalupe as coach).

Questions for Reflection

1. Does the idea of surrender to God seem calming or does it leave you feeling upset and worried? How can you find peace in surrender?
2. What is God inviting you to surrender totally to him right now?

3. After surrendering something to God, do you find yourself trying to take control again, worried that things will not turn out unless you orchestrate them yourself? Can you lay your burdens down at the feet of God once and for all and leave things to him?

Questions for Conversation

1. What is something you fear? How is the Lord inviting you to surrender that fear to him?
2. How would your life look different if you lived in complete surrender to Divine Providence? How would total trust in God change your day to day life as a Catholic woman?
3. Are you competing well and running the race like St. Paul? What are some practices that you have found helpful in your journey to surrender to the will of God?

Come Holy Spirit, living in Mary. When I am consumed by worry, transform this worry into trust and whole hearted surrender. When I'm tempted to snatch back my plans, hopes, and dreams, remind me that they rest secure in your hands, God. When I'm confused by your will and nervous toward your plan, give me the courage and fortitude to pray for trust in your Divine Providence. Amen.

A Letter to the Woman Getting Ready for the First Date

"You learn to speak by speaking, to study by studying, to run by running, to work by working, and just so, you learn to love by loving. All those who think to learn in any other way deceive themselves."

—St. Francis de Sales

I'll forever remember my first date with my now husband, Joseph. He picked me up from my parents' house in his maroon pickup truck and drove us to the county fair. We wandered among rows of photography displays and barnyard animals getting to know each other. Then, we grabbed pizza for dinner before he dropped me back off for the night. It was simple, fun delightful. I was excited, and nervous.

It was my *first* first date. No one had ever asked me out before Joseph came along. It was also my last first date, and I couldn't have been happier.

Maybe you're excited for your first ever first date too. I know exactly what that feels like. Or maybe you're getting ready for one of many first dates that you've been on, and you're learning more about yourself and what you value in a date and in a relationship. Regardless of whether this is your first ever first date or the twentieth first date, I can't wait to introduce you to Patty and her wisdom that she shares in this letter.

Patty is a woman who I've gotten to know through her genuine and honest writing about her dating experience as a Catholic woman. I've long admired her practical advice and kind encouragement that she's given to Catholics who dive into the world of dating.

If you're nervously getting ready for your first date, sister, this letter is for you.

Dear sister,

You're deciding what outfit to put together with accessories that add just the right touch without being too much. Feeling confident, you style your hair, spray a few wisps of your go-to perfume, and apply your favorite lipstick before grabbing your purse and car keys to head out the door.

Driving to the meeting place, your stomach is an equal mix of nerves, excitement, and anxiety. You park the car and take one final approving look at yourself before heading inside.

As you pull the handle of the door to the restaurant, you say a little prayer: Holy Spirit, fill me with your peace. Help me to just be myself. Make it abundantly clear if I should be open to something with this man.

And you walk in. You're going on your first date.

I don't know if this is your first date after years of no dates or just really bad ones. Perhaps this is your first date after a painful breakup, your divorce and annulment, or the death of your husband.

First dates can be anything on the spectrum from thrilling to awful.

If we were real-life friends, I would want to leave with you a few encouraging reminders as you are preparing to go on that first date. These things I share from my heart to yours have become my battle cries, anthems if you will, to remind me of the truths about myself, my life, and how Jesus looks at me. They are things I think all of us women need to be reminded of from time to time.

Heaven knows, I've had to learn these truths and apply them in my own life. I've made plenty of mistakes and choices when it came to dating and healthy relationships, but I am so grateful for what I have learned about myself and what God has taught me.

First, be open, show up, and live your life. Sweet friend, can I tell you something very important? You already have everything you need to live a rich, meaningful life. Just be open and show up to live your life.

This first date you are about to go on has the potential to be the beginning of a great relationship. It could also go down in complete flames. Regardless of this first date (or future ones!), you already have all that you need to live a beautiful life. Your life begins right now, not when you are in a serious relationship with a man. Be open to all the new possibilities your life holds for you right now. This could mean following creative dreams, investing in hobbies you want to develop, going on dates and practicing healthy dating, traveling, and taking care of your physical body.

Let this become your anthem! Cheer yourself onward! Your single season of life does not mean your life will be any less rich or beautiful. The energy and attitude we bring to life is what shapes how we live it. So live well, sister! Be open to all the possibilities (and yes all the dates!). Show up for the beautiful adventure that is your life!

Second, don't be afraid to ask Jesus to come surprise you. Last spring, I was fresh off my first mature, grownup break-up. While I was at peace with my decision to end things, I still looked with trepidation to my future and how to rectify the deepest desires of my heart.

I began to pray and ask Jesus to come surprise me. Daily, often in the car, I would simply pour out my heart: "Jesus, would you just come and surprise me in every area of my life? In my job and career, my creative dreams and pursuits, in dating and the desire for marriage, etc.; Jesus, just come and surprise me in every area of life."

I know that might sound like a strange thing to say to a woman preparing for a first date. Here is why I offer it to you. When it came to love and relationships in my life, it was always about my grasping and striving for a significant relationship. I wanted a relationship, and so I did everything in my power (and by my striving!) to make it happen. The problem is that striving and grasping are not what Jesus wants for me in my own vocational discernment.

Love is a pure gift, and from what I have gathered from this little prayer in my heart, it will play out as a natural, wonderful surprise.

Praying this way opened my clenched fists to Jesus and loosened my iron grip of control. It helped me to get out of the way and trust Jesus in a deeper way with the desires I have for marriage and a family someday. Ask Jesus to come and surprise you in every area of your life, but be bold and even ask him to come surprise you in dating, love, and relationships.

I do not offer this prayer to you as a trite way to say something like "Well, just pray in this particular way and then Jesus will deliver you Mr. Tall, Dark, and Handsome." Remember, Jesus is not our divine vending machine. Realizing this helped me let go of my timeline and practice trusting God's timeline for my life more deeply and took the energy and focus off needing to make something happen.

I hope you had a wonderful, fun time on your first date, that you laughed deeply, ate some delicious food, and felt comfortable enough to accept an offer for a second date.

Whether your first date was a first rate success or disaster, I want you to show up as your authentic self and radiate your unique joy and beauty.

My hope and prayer for you is that you will show up and be open to living your life right now, here in the present moment.

Jesus has good plans for your life. We can trust our hopes and dreams to him.

Patty Breen

Patty Breen has been working in lay ministry for over ten years and is a writer for Blessed is She. *A Midwestern girl from the mitten state, Patty finds joy in running, strong cups of coffee, Ignatian spirituality, and writing. She is passionate about messy conversations at the intersection of faith, culture, and ministry.*

Questions for Reflection

1. Have you ever been tempted to believe that your life will only begin when you enter a romantic relationship, or after you discern your vocation? How can you live fully alive in the present moment?

2. Are you open to letting Christ surprise you, or are you holding tightly to your own plans and not surrendering everything (including your love life) over to him? What is holding you back from his surprises?

3. Have you treated Christ like a divine vending machine, believing that if you put just the right things in (like time in prayer, volunteering in your community, going to Mass, etc.) that he'll give you just what you want? How can you reject this mentality and instead approach your relationship with Christ in a spirit of receptivity?

Questions for Conversation

1. How do you define a good first date? Where would you go, what would you do, and what would you talk about with someone on that first date?

2. What are some bold prayers you can start praying when it comes to your love life? Is there anything holding you back from those bold prayers?

3. Although they can leave you cringing, disappointing first dates allow you to find out what you are looking for on a date and in a relationship. What are some lessons you've learned from bad first date experiences?

Come Holy Spirit, living in Mary. Give me the grace to surrender every aspect of my life over to your divine will. When I'm tempted to think that a first date, a relationship, or even my discerned vocation will bring complete satisfaction in my life, remind me that true and complete satisfaction only comes from you, Lord. Amen.

A Letter to the Woman Who Loves Someone Addicted to Pornography

"There is no dignity when the human dimension is eliminated from the person. In short, the problem with pornography is not that it shows too much of the person, but that it shows far too little."

—Pope St. John Paul II

We have a pornography problem. A prominent pornography website sees more than 115 million visitors every day.[4] The global pornography industry revenue is estimated to be $97 billion annually.[5] When the American Academy for Matrimonial Lawyers interviewed 350 divorce attorneys, the attorneys reported that internet pornography played a prominent role in 56 percent of their divorce cases.[6]

---

[4]   "Pornhub's Annual Report: Can You Guess 2019's Top Searched Porn Terms?" Fight the New Drug, December 17, 2019, https://fightthenewdrug.org/2019-pornhub-annual-report/.

[5]   "Every Day, Millions Of People Watch Porn. How Does This Impact Society?" Fight the New Drug, May 26, 2020, https://fightthenewdrug.org/what-is-the-collective-impact-of-millions-of-people-watching-porn/.

[6]   "National Review: Getting Serious On Pornography," NPR, March 31, 2020, https://www.npr.org/templates/story/story.php?storyId=125382361.

But maybe these statistics and numbers aren't just statistics and numbers to you. Maybe those numbers hit close to your home and close to your heart because you know someone and love someone who struggles with an addiction to pornography—and it's breaking your heart.

What can you do to help someone in your life who battles against pornography? If your boyfriend, fiancé, or husband is using pornography, you may feel angry, confused, and deceived. But to make the situation even worse, pornography addiction is something we don't talk enough about in today's society. Conversations about the impact that pornography has on our hearts, brains, and relationships are few and far between.

Pornography isn't an easy topic to talk about. But Amanda is a woman who is breaking the silence around this issue, and I couldn't be more grateful for her witness and her honesty. In this letter, she shares her experience of navigating her husband's addiction to pornography and desiring hope, healing, and freedom for him.

If you're wrestling with how to love someone in your life who is addicted to pornography, sister, this letter is for you.

Dear sister,

I stood at the kitchen island, frozen in shock, as rage began to bubble up inside me. Jonathan had just dropped the massive bomb on me that he'd been living a secret life addicted to pornography and masturbation for the first seven and half years of our marriage.

Fight and flight instincts were sparring to win my first reaction. And then out it came: "I HATE YOU! GET THE HELL OUT OF MY HOUSE YOU LIAR!"

My husband stood there, eyes downcast and crying. He looked like the smallest man I'd ever seen. I ran upstairs and grabbed hangers with his clothes on them and threw them down the stairs until they were gone. I bagged up his toiletries in a duffel bag and tossed them down while screaming that I never wanted to see him again.

He didn't protest. I heard the garage door shut and I slunk down against the wall, trying to make sense of this. Mercifully, our two girls who were three and one at the time were napping that day and hadn't witnessed this blow-out of a fight.

Jonathan and I had talked about pornography and masturbation when we were dating. He revealed that it had been a struggle of his but he was leaving it firmly in the past. Every single month since we had married on October 22, 2011, we would even check in about it and it was always A-OK. Until it wasn't.

I called a neighbor who I knew had faced similar struggles in her marriage. As we talked, I felt my anger and desire to hurt Jonathan dissipate. My husband was not the enemy here. It was Satan. She invited me to courageously link arms with the entirety of heaven and be willing to battle *for* my husband's freedom as he was trapped behind enemy lines.

For my husband, this was an addiction. It wasn't something he was in control of and could pray away. While I'd been in the dark about it for those first seven years of our marriage, I clearly saw the effects: rage, self-hatred, self-harm, low self-esteem, and depression. He was miserable and spoke up that day as a plea for help.

I texted Jonathan that I wanted to meet him to talk. My neighbor graciously offered to put my kids to sleep and told me to stay out talking to Jonathan as late as I needed.

He cried and apologized extensively. I told him I was in this for the long haul, that I wasn't going to give up on him, and that we, together with Jesus and Our Lady, would fight for his freedom. We laid out boundaries, identified weak spots, discussed temptations, and more or less designed our battle plans for the war.

We went home together, hung up my husband's clothes, put his toiletries back in the drawer, and prepared for a long and windy road ahead. It was a path I knew would bring me hurt. But I also knew that if we clung to Jesus, this cross had the power to carry us to heaven.

It's been two years since that fateful day, and we've learned a lot. There have been relapses, but they're farther and fewer between as we learn more about addiction and modify our lifestyles to support sobriety.

Our family isn't alone in this struggle. Pornography and masturbation are an alarmingly common struggle many holy Catholic marriages face. But no one talks about it.

Women stay silent, not wanting to expose their husbands' struggles and the ugly reality of their married life. Their husbands don't know where to turn because it seems like everyone they know also struggles yet hides.

But here's what I will leave you with my dear sisters: this battle is with the enemy of our souls. The more darkness that surrounds the battle, the greater the likelihood that it will be lost. Jesus desires to bring light into the darkness. Practically, this can mean many things. But staying silent, suffering alone, and keeping the battle private between you and your husband isn't one of them.

If your husband is using pornography and masturbating, you need truth tellers in your life. Women who will be a safe haven to talk and pray with along the journey. Without my neighbor that day, it's possible I would've given up on my marriage. If you don't know anyone in real life to turn to, there are online communities too.

You and your spouse need to learn about addiction. For many men, it's not just a struggle but an addiction. Until you treat it for what it is, nearly all efforts will be in vain. Men's accountability groups, prayer, filtering software, and confession will *not* be enough for an addict. God uses grace and nature. Sexaholics Anonymous needs to be part of the healing process because of the scientifically proven path to recovery it provides.

My dear sister, you need to take care of yourself emotionally. You don't need details about your husband's searches or what he has watched. Please, do *not* pursue these details or watch pornography to see what your husband is up to. This is only ammo for Satan to use against you and torment you mentally. If you start to get obsessive, wondering what your husband is up to constantly, and feeling like *you* have to keep tabs on your spouse at all times, it's time to get counseling. It's extremely common for spouses of addicts to experience PTSD, and you do not need to suffer unnecessarily.

You are enough. Your spouse's addiction isn't about you. It's not a reflection on your attractiveness, worth, weight, wrinkles, stretch marks, sexual drive (or lack of), past mistakes, or spiritual life.

If you aren't yet married and find out your boyfriend or fiancé is addicted to pornography and masturbation, you need to be clear that he needs to seek help immediately. An addict who is actively using is not free to give himself to another. Full knowledge on your end and sobriety on his end is a necessary condition of entering into a sacrament. You can avoid a whole lot of pain by facing the addiction head on as you discern marriage.

Lastly, I invite you to link arms with me and all of heaven, dear sister, as we battle for the souls of all those addicted to pornography and masturbation. The enemy has used this to destroy many souls and marriages.

Personally, I'm on a search and rescue mission with Jesus to assist him as he sets people free. Join me in this fight. We're stronger together.

Amanda

Amanda Teixeira hails from Omaha, Nebraska. She is a wife, mother, and co-founder of WalletWin, a personal finance education company. Amanda is a nationally sought after speaker and writer on the topics of finances, leadership, and femininity. Before launching WalletWin, she served nine years as a staff member with FOCUS. When she isn't running her business, Amanda can be found having spontaneous dance parties or exploring the outdoors with her husband, Jonathan, daughters Josephine, Charlotte, and Eleanor, and their beloved Labrador retriever, Wrigley.

Questions for Reflection

1. Have you taken time to grieve the losses and pain you've experienced because of your husband, fiancé, or boyfriend's pornography addiction? Can you be honest about that grief in prayer with God?

2. If someone you love is addicted to pornography, their addiction isn't your fault. Do you believe this statement?

3. Do you feel alone and isolated in this experience of loving someone with an addiction to pornography? How can you seek out community and support in this journey?

Questions for Conversation

1. What are some boundaries you've put in place during your experience loving someone who is addicted to pornography? How have those boundaries aided this healing process?

2. How can you do battle with all of heaven for the souls of those addicted to pornography and masturbation?

3. Who are women who can journey alongside you and support you and can speak truth into this situation?

Come Holy Spirit, living in Mary. Strengthen me as I work to will the good of someone I love who is addicted to pornography. When I feel ashamed, bring your light. When I feel discouraged, bring your hope. When I feel broken, bring your healing and truth. Remind me that I am good, your beloved daughter, and grant me the grace of wisdom and courage. Amen.

A Letter to the Woman Discerning Marriage

"Love is never something readymade, something merely 'given' to man and woman; it is always at the same time a 'task' which they are set. Love should be seen as something which in a sense never 'is' but is always only 'becoming,' and what it becomes depends upon the contributions of both persons and the depth of their commitment."

—Pope St. John Paul II

I'm a fan of hopelessly sappy romantic comedies, much to my husband's chagrin. But even before I started dating Joseph, I started to realize that love isn't what they sell us in romantic comedies. It's something different and better than anything we find in a Hallmark Christmas movie. True love is willing the good of the other and diving deep into sacrificial love. True love is what we see when we gaze upon Christ on the crucifix.

But what does it mean to discern loving someone through the vocation of marriage?

Emily is a fellow lover of those same romantic movies, as you'll soon find out. But more important than knowing that she's a woman I could sit with on a couch, laughing (and crying!) our way through our fair share of romantic comedies,

Emily is an incredible witness to the reality of friendship and love in a God centered marriage with her husband.

As you discern God's will in your life, I know her wisdom in this letter can be a source of encouragement and hope.

If you hear the Lord calling you to the vocation of marriage, sister, this letter is for you.

Dear sister,

As I sit here writing this, I have Jane Austen's *Emma* in my lap, and I'm fresh off of an annual watching of the movie that tells us not to over-romanticize love by over-romanticizing love: *Sleepless in Seattle*. Next to me is my husband of almost three years, snoring loudly and taking up more than his fair share of the bed, certainly a stark contrast to the romantic image of these stories! And yet, I still think we have a better love story than any author or movie producer could write.

I remember my mom and me talking about rom-coms when I was a preteen and how they weren't realistic. She warned me that true love isn't like that at all. I replied, "No, it'll be better, because it will be real!" Somehow, twelve-year-old me got it right. Sister, marriage (or love for that matter) isn't like it is in the movies. It's simple. It's quiet. And it's amazing.

My husband, Aaron, and I met in the most unfanciful of ways; we attended our soon-to-be college's Accepted Student Day, and a mutual friend introduced us. I honestly barely remember the encounter, though now I look at a grainy photo of us captured that day by the college's photographer and smile at those two kids who didn't know they'd just met their spouse.

We became friends our freshman year out of convenience. My husband, never the socialite, was happy to be swept into the exuberant friend circle which I also happened to fall into. Then, throughout that first semester, the friend group slowly dwindled until it was just us.

The one thing we had in common was going to daily Mass together. My husband tells me now that I was what convinced him to go to Mass since he had been prepared to be the only person interested in faith at the school. Slowly, after sitting next to the only other person under the age of sixty at Mass, we just naturally became friends. This blossoming of our friendship echoes the rest of our relationship; it was quiet and just kind of happened without us even knowing it. Our personalities just worked really well together. It wasn't long until we were best friends without even really trying to be.

Of course, everyone instantly began to assume we were dating because we were together all the time. It became the running joke around campus that we were going to get married someday. We were the only two who didn't buy into it! I'd always protest that he was like a brother to me. I would even tell him about all the guys I had crushes on and would ask for his advice. I thought that our friendship was too important to risk on a relationship.

Everything changed one night during sophomore year. I was trying to fall asleep one night and thinking about how much of a gentleman Aaron was. He was kind, respectful, and religious. What more could I want in a guy? I decided then and there that I wanted to marry a guy like him. Suddenly, I sat straight up in bed. Why didn't I just marry Aaron?

I went from purely platonic to marriage-minded in an instant, which I still find hilarious. Forget about dating! There was no hesitation, no doubt. Aaron was my best friend, and I wanted to marry him. Thankfully, he'd started to develop a similar interest in me, though his feelings had started months before. We finally discovered our mutual secret by revealing it in confidence to the same friend within forty-eight hours of each other. She had been sworn to secrecy by us both, but only lasted about two hours before blurting out to me, "I lied, I do know something you don't know. Aaron likes you too. But act normal, because here he comes!" Yeah, act normal. After a series of misadventures that included trying to keep from bouncing up and down for joy during a somber 9/11 memorial service and Aaron banging his head against the wall while trying to work up the courage, he finally asked me out.

Within an hour of making our relationship official, Aaron asked me to go pray with him up at the college chapel to start our relationship off with God. I remember him asking God to be with us no matter where our relationship would go and feeling like my heart was going to burst with joy for the privilege of getting to love this incredibly devout man.

God certainly has been with us. He was with us two weeks later when we first started talking about marrying each other. Then, a year and a half later, we began long distance dating. A year after that, Aaron asked me to marry him in the same chapel that we prayed in to begin our relationship. And finally, God was present ten months after our engagement when we got married in the same chapel.

Throughout our journey, I learned how simple romance can really be. I grew up on classic romance novels and romantic movies, and I thought love was going to be a lightning bolt with some grand gesture that would take my breath away. Instead, my love story reminds me of God's voice to the prophet Elijah: still and small.

I want to encourage you not to believe what Hollywood says marriage and love should be. This is what marriage is: it's not being able to sleep when the other person isn't there. It's being able to have a whole conversation with your spouse in public without saying a word. Sometimes, marriage is having your husband buy his own Valentine's Day candy because he has a coupon and works closer to the store. Marriage isn't a continual high; it's a slow burn that fills every part of you with a joy that lasts forever.

Don't shy away from a relationship just because it doesn't feel like fireworks. Love can develop in so many ways. From personal experience, a relationship rooted in friendship may feel anticlimactic, but it gives you a foundation to love long past the end of the "honeymoon phase." As I told Aaron the other day, at the very worst, I get to be married to my best friend for the rest of my life. Counting love out of it (though I love him an incredible amount), that's still a pretty awesome future!

If you are discerning your call to marriage, I would implore you to prepare your heart and practice loving by just being a good friend. If you're feeling like your prince will never come, take a look around you and see who God might be hiding in plain sight for you.

Listen to the still, small voice. You'll be surprised where (and to whom) it will take you, but I promise it will always lead you towards joy.

Emily

Emily Ricci is the owner and founder of Gloriam Marketing, LLC, a Catholic marketing and creative agency that works with churches and Catholic organizations on projects that promote their ministries and Christ. She is also the Assistant Director of Digital Communications at her alma mater and an adjunct professor of Religious Studies. Emily is married to her college sweetheart, Aaron, and enjoys reading, knitting, and playing guitar in her spare time.

Questions for Reflection

1. Do you believe God is calling you to the vocation of marriage? Are you ready to surrender your plans and ideas for marriage and trust God on this journey to the altar?
2. No person can satisfy us—not even a spouse! Only God can bring total and complete fulfillment into our lives. How can you find satisfaction in Christ while you discern his calling for your life?
3. How are you listening to the still, small voice of God when it comes to discerning your vocation?

Questions for Conversation

1. What are some stereotypes about romance, dating, and marriage that you have thanks to popular movies, books, and shows? Where do those stereotypes fall flat?

2. Marriage isn't a continual high, and you'll experience disagreements and conflicts. What are some ways that you can prepare yourself to communicate your thoughts and emotions now while you discern a vocation to marriage?

3. How can becoming a better friend prepare you for marriage?

Come Holy Spirit, living in Mary. As I discern your will in my life in regards to my vocation, help me become attuned to your still, small voice. Give me the grace to become a better listener and a better friend. But most of all, help me to surrender my plans over to you and be fully receptive to your will in my life. Amen.

A Letter to the Woman Discerning Adoption

"Adopting children, regarding and treating them as one's own children, means recognizing that the relationship between parents and children is not measured only by genetic standards. Procreative love is first and foremost a gift of self. There is a form of 'procreation' which occurs through acceptance, concern, and devotion."

—Pope St. John Paul II

When I was experiencing secondary infertility after losing our son to miscarriage, there was one line at every Catholic wedding I'd attend that would leave me feeling empty and broken: "Be fruitful and multiply." It felt like a knife twisting in my heart, and it left me wondering if my infertility meant that my marriage couldn't be fruitful.

During that season of my life, passages from John chapter fifteen were incredibly consoling. Christ says that he is the vine and we are the branches. When we abide and rest with the Lord, we'll bear fruit, and that fruit will remain. Christ invites all of us to bear fruit.

Mary is a woman who has taught me about what bearing fruit looks like in different seasons. In conversations with her, I've learned about the beauty of spiritual maternity, what it looks like to find healing from wounds, and how to discern if God is calling you to grow your family through adoption.

If you're desiring to learn whether or not God is calling you and your family to bear fruit through adoption, sister, this letter is for you.

Dear sister,

"We made a cute one," I laughingly uttered to my husband, Chris, as our daughter skipped off in front of us with an adorable smile while hollering "Come get me!" during one of our daily walks. It's ironic because we didn't make Bella in the traditional sense of the word often used by parents. As we had struggled to get pregnant month after month, I had struggled to recognize God's love for me until he began to show up in ways I wasn't expecting. She did not grow in my belly, nor does she share our ethnicity or physical attributes, but we have shaped her in ways that no other two people could have. And that is really beautiful. Infertility started out as an experience that would consistently rob us of peace and hope with each passing month, but it ended up delivering us one of our most precious joys, and her name is Isabella.

Like most people do, I assumed children would "just happen" after I got married and when the timing was right. That's generally what we see happening around us, especially in our beautiful Catholic culture. But Chris and I were working very hard with a handful of (Church approved) medical professionals for that one priceless conception that just would not come. I was confused because I was confident in my discerned vocation as wife and mother. I was broken-hearted because in the absence of a pregnancy, one of the many wonderful things God has uniquely created woman for, I felt forgotten by him.

About two and a half years into infertility, I had a pretty rough day that resulted from my first and only false positive pregnancy test. It felt like a cruel joke. My anger reached a new level and a new direction, pointing directly at the crucifix hanging on my wall. I asked him, "How could you do this to me?" He returned with, "You say that you love me. Do you mean it?" These ten words struck me to my core as I recognized that loving him meant taking a leap of faith and trusting the presence of his arms to catch me as I dropped, even when I couldn't see his hands and even if it wasn't how I chose to fall.

Everything changed for me on that day as I began to make the difficult daily decision to love and trust God, even as I was hurting deeply and did not yet agree with this route to holiness, or happiness. Adoption had been discussed several times up until that point, especially because Chris had been ready to start the process. I had dragged my feet because I perceived beginning the adoption process to mean accepting defeat, but that was just another way of saying that I wasn't ready to part with my sense of control. When I finally chose to hand it over to God, who was waiting patiently to give me the desires of my heart, I was scared, but I was ready to start the process and meet the child he had always had in mind for us.

At this point, we were sure of three things: we were called to be parents now or soon, we weren't getting pregnant, and in vitro fertilization was not an option.

Not every infertile couple is called to adoption, but God was clearly leading us there. Yet even as we eagerly stepped into the process, we both had some understandable fears beyond those typically associated with becoming new parents. We worried that we might not feel like he or she would be one of our own. We worried about potential unknown health issues. We worried about how others might treat us and our new baby, especially into adolescence. We worried about whether or not we would be able to afford to adopt a brother or sister.

There will always be something to worry about, but there is a place on the cross of Christ to place every single one of those fears. Almost one full year later, our social worker presented Bella's birth mother's case to us—the third or fourth birth mother who was brought to us. With a lot of prayer and despite having plenty to be anxious about, I felt a distinct peace about this one as I said to Chris, "Our daughter is our daughter no matter the cost."

About two months later, we held our very own baby girl in our arms without one doubt or sense of worry. We also had a new incredible respect for birth mothers who are often unsung heroes. The idea that Bella wouldn't feel like our own because I didn't carry her and because she doesn't share our DNA felt like a distant dream that faded into the background well before she was even born. We encountered plenty of unexpected challenges throughout the process, but they mattered little in comparison to finally meeting our daughter. There will certainly be more unique trials which will present themselves as she ages, and we will do our best to address those with confidence through prayer like any other family would. No future experience could make our ability to be her parents any less of a privilege.

If I'm being honest, I never imagined how complete an adopted child would make our family—but God is impressive like that. We can trust that he not only knows the desires of our hearts but makes those his desires as well. His gifts are abundant, and his generosity is even further displayed in the many ways Bella's personality resembles our personalities. It has been a sweet surprise to hear both strangers and friends comment on how much she looks like us as she gets older and develops her own little combinations of Chris and me. From his design of our little family and the struggle we endured to conform to it to Bella's specific features contributed by her birth parents, God has perfectly shaped our tribe—and we think he made a pretty awesome one.

May God bless you,

Mary G. Bruno

Mary is a wife and adoptive mother who loves playing sports and eating chocolate. She is the creator of Taking Back the Terms, an outreach that helps to educate and motivate women of all ages, couples, and priests about authentic and restorative women's healthcare via NFP/ fertility awareness. Two of her objectives are to help women identify early risk factors for infertility and to provide others with knowledge of healthier and more cost effective alternatives to birth control and IVF. A late diagnosis, subsequent infertility, and love of her Catholic faith has inspired this mission. She is a Creighton Practitioner, speaker, writer, rapper, podcaster, and is currently writing her first book. Find her at MaryGBruno.com.

Questions for Reflection

1. Is God calling you to discern adoption? What are some ways that you have heard that call in prayer and throughout your daily life?
2. How can you surrender your plans for your family to the Lord? Do you trust that he loves you and has good plans in store?
3. What are some fears that you have about discerning adoption? How can God bring peace to those fears?

Questions for Conversation

1. Has God been opening or closing doors in your discernment of adoption?
2. How has God brought peace and hope out of a trying situation in your own life?
3. Has someone in your life witnessed to the beauty of life and love through adoption? How has their witness impacted your story?

Come Holy Spirit, living in Mary. You've called each and every one of us to bear fruit in our lives, and that fruit will look different in each of our stories. Today, I especially pray for families who you are inviting to grow through adoption. Give them courage, hope, and peace in this discernment. If you're calling my family to discern adoption, I surrender my plans for my family today and ask for the grace to trust the good plans you have in store. Amen.

A Letter to the Woman at Home with Kids

"Stay where you are. Find your own Calcutta. Find the sick, the suffering, and the lonely, right where you are."
—St. Teresa of Calcutta

When someone asks you what you do during the day as a stay-at-home mom, are you tempted to say that you "just" stay home? We live in a society that demands that we prove our worth by our productivity and the figures on our paychecks, which can leave women who stay at home with their family feeling less-than. But that couldn't be further from the truth.

If you're a woman and mother who stays home, defending your choice to stay at home with your children may be a situation all too familiar to you. Despite your discernment and knowledge of what works best for your family, you may know what it feels like to fend off comments from family, friends, and strangers. It's wonderful to be able to set your own routine, be with your kids, and not have to worry about work deadlines. But you may also be battling feelings of isolation and loneliness and longing for conversations with someone who can share adult thoughts.

If you're staying at home and raising a family, you need to meet Emily. She brings honesty and humor to the conversation about being a stay-at-home mom. I first met Emily through her blog and social media, but she's quickly become a friend, and I love talking about everything from fashion to politics with her. I've been blessed by the way she lives out her unique feminine genius by fostering community and cultivating meaningful conversation among women.

If you're spending time at home with your little ones and finding yourself battling insecurities, sister, this letter is for you.

Dear sister,

It had been the worst day. Somewhere in the world there was a military crisis and, as usual, my boss was in high demand. I was in the midst of coordinating travel plans, speaking engagements, and the day-to-day office affairs. My email inbox was flooded with media requests from our communication department for my boss to appear on Fox News, do radio shows, and give quotes for news articles. It was my job to vet, confirm, or deny them in less than an hour. It was a normal day really, no different than a million other days I'd tackled over the previous five years.

But that day was different. That day I was also a mom. This military skirmish was competing with my daughter's cluster feeding and nap strike, and I could feel anger bubbling up inside me with every new email and phone call. A situation I had learned to navigate with a calm professionalism was turning me inside out, and it wasn't the first time this had happened since I returned after maternity leave.

"How does any of this matter when my baby needs me?" I screamed internally.

I had definitely expected some tension as I returned to work as a new mom, but now it seemed that juggling motherhood and a career was going to cost me my sanity. No one deserved that, not me, my baby, my husband, or my boss.

It was a situation I never saw coming. I grew up with a stay-at-home mom, and all of my friends from childhood had moms at home as well. Seeing and living the benefits of having a mom at home had set my mind on doing the same one day. But life rarely turns out how you imagined it would when you were fifteen. When I graduated college, I found myself jumping at an internship opportunity in DC, an unexpected choice considering I had majored in architecture and hated politics.

God had quite the adventure in store for me, much to my delight. My internship turned into an incredible job that fed my desire to change the culture. My boss was a rare person who saw it as his responsibility to cultivate the talent of those in his employ. As we got to know each other, he began to trust me with larger responsibilities, editing his speeches and writings, and advising him on matters of office administration. Over time, we developed a father/daughter-like relationship. The job was delightfully challenging, stimulating, and fulfilling. It was an all-around dream.

Then one day I met a boy, and that boy and I fell in love. And as tends to happen in such circumstances, we got married and were expecting our first child within three months.

By this point, the idea of quitting my job to stay home with my child had been completely wiped from my mind. Financially, DC is not conducive to raising a family on one income. Plus I loved my job, and my boss graciously worked out a flexible schedule so I could balance being a mom with work as best I could.

It wasn't long after I returned that I began to lose my peace, and that rough day was the final straw. My husband and I re-crunched our finances that night and realized I could stay home without going bankrupt. I sat down in my boss's office in tears and told him my decision. He teared up as well but told me he was proud of me. As much as we'd miss each other, this was the right thing to do.

The relief upon going from working two jobs to just one was immediate. I could give my daughter the undivided attention I wanted and focus more intentionally on our home and marriage. In spite of that, deep feelings of insecurity began to creep in.

We went to a friend's annual Halloween party a year after I had quit attended by people who work in various capacities in the conservative movement and who were all supportive of stay-at-home moms. By now, our son had joined our family, and he came along as part of my costume. When the host asked me how I was doing, I uncharacteristically stuttered out a response about cleaning diaper blowouts and wiping snotty noses. I suddenly felt utterly small and insecure in a room full of people whose jobs shaped public policy, a world I had been very much a part of not long before. I cried from embarrassment on the way home.

That I had made the right decision wasn't a question. The peace and calm I felt after I quit was undeniable. The joy of being a mom to my babies without any competition was palpable. It hadn't occurred to me that just making the right decision wasn't enough, that I would now have to own it and give an authentic and joyful witness to a world that saw my choice as a waste and a shame. I spent time talking with friends who had made the same decision, reading others' experiences, and especially time in prayer, drawing the encouragement and affirmation I needed to walk boldly into this new life.

Even as I embraced my choice, there was still something missing. The transition from working full time with all its perks to managing tantrums, nap times, and picky appetites was a bit of a shock. I needed a creative outlet, something that would stretch me intellectually even while I was being stretched every other way.

As I settled into the rhythm of life at home, I realized that I had time to cultivate a passion that had always been kept on the back burner: writing. From high school to architecture to my time in DC, I could see where God had planted a love for encouraging others, connecting ideas, and building community through the written word, and how he used each of those experiences to help me learn to write well. It was as though God was just waiting for my world to shrink to the four walls of our teeny apartment so I would have the freedom and the desire to let what he had planted bloom.

My physical world has gotten very small, but it is the very thing that enabled me to write this letter to you now, giving me the opportunity to encourage and affirm you even while we will probably never meet.

Just like any vocation God could have called me to, being a stay-at-home mom has stretched me and tested me at the same time it fulfills me and blesses me and my family. Every day, the mere fact that my children exist and I am home with them forces me to be a better person. It is a beautiful challenge and an incredibly important job. The absolute last thing I would call it is limiting. It has broadened the gifts and talents I have used my whole life in the most pleasantly surprising ways.

If you are wondering whether the stay-at-home mom life is for you, the test is simple: interior peace.

Whether at work or in the home, where do you find it? That is where you are meant to be. Say yes, and watch God open doors you'll never have expected.

In solidarity,

Emily

Emily Frase is a south Louisiana native living outside DC with her Wisconsin-born husband, Nick, and their two cherubs. After five years working in the political arena, she left to run her own rat race at home and was amazed at how well working with politicians prepared her for toddlers. She is passionate about a gloves-off approach to NFP education and promotes honest conversations about motherhood and faithful living through her blog, Total Whine.

Questions for Reflection

1. What circumstances and decisions are playing a part in your discernment to stay at home with your children?
2. If you stay at home with your children, have you ever experienced insecurity in that decision? Where have you found encouragement and affirmation in this decision to stay home?
3. Is there a creative outlet that you're able to invest in during your time at home with kids?

Questions for Conversation

1. Have you found interior peace in your discernment to stay at home and raise your children?
2. What are ways that family, friends, and society can better support women who stay at home with their children?
3. What talents and gifts of yours have been broadened as you stay at home with your kids?

Come Holy Spirit, living in Mary. As I spend days with my children at home, reveal to me in your still, quiet voice where you desire me to grow. Open my eyes to the little ways you desire to encounter me within the ordinary day-to-day here with my family. Bring peace and joy to these moments and equip me to grow into the woman and mother you've created me to be. Amen.

A Letter to the Woman Who's a Working Mom

"Thank you, women who work! You are present and active in every area of life—social, economic, cultural, artistic, and political. In this way you make an indispensable contribution to the growth of a culture which unites reason and feeling, to a model of life ever open to the sense of 'mystery,' to the establishment of economic and political structures ever more worthy of humanity."
—Pope St. John Paul II

In my first year as a working mom, I had a haunting feeling that I wasn't giving anyone my best. When I was at work, I was thinking about my daughter and what needed to be done at home. When I was with my daughter, I found myself thinking about what needed to be done on different projects or deadlines that were approaching. It felt like I was existing in a constant state of conflict. That's when I met JoAnna.

I've never met a woman so passionate about journeying alongside working mothers as JoAnna. Her wisdom and advice have helped me multiple times during my discernment of job situations.

JoAnna strives to create community with other working mothers. Her accompaniment and encouragement helps women who are navigating the reality of working and mothering know that they're not alone.

If you're a working mom and feel like you're being pulled in different directions all at the same time, sister, this letter is for you.

Dear sister,

I know how conflicted you feel each and every day. You work hard so that your children will have a safe home, good healthcare, plenty to eat, and clean clothes to wear. I know how hard you work so that your husband doesn't have to shoulder the heavy burden of being the only breadwinner. I know you take pride in your professional accomplishments and how hard you work to serve your community using the talents God has given you.

But I also know that you wish you could spend more time at home, taking care of the chores that constantly pile up and that always seem to go undone. You wish you could spend more time with your kids instead of just the rushed mornings, a few hours in the evening, and the weekends that go by too fast. I know that the guilt is always hovering at the periphery, trying to steal the moments of joy you do take in your children, your family, or your work.

Mama, you are not alone when you feel torn in nine different directions every day. It sometimes feels like an impossible juggling act and any minute one or all of those balls you have in the air will come crashing down around you.

Sometimes they do. Maybe an illness derails a long-awaited family holiday, a broken down vehicle means a planned vacation won't happen, or an emergency at work causes you to miss your child's event.

Feeling guilty and stressed out while balancing all of your competing priorities does not mean that you have made the wrong choice in your decision to work. No life is free from guilt and stress, and no mother is always free from wishing that she had more time to spend with her family, whether it is because she is working or because she has a never-ending to-do list at home.

St. Gianna Beretta Molla, in a letter to she wrote to her husband while she was on vacation from her job with their young children and he had to remain at home to work, said, "Dear Pietro, how beautiful it is to be able to stay with them day and night, to watch and enjoy them all of the time. I can imagine how disappointed you must be when you come home in the evening and they are already in bed. It doesn't seem real to them to have their Mamma all to themselves all of the time. Gigetto [a nickname for her oldest son, Pierluigi]—maybe because he's going to preschool—does nothing but call to me, and he would like nothing better than to have me all to himself."[7]

St. Gianna loved her work as a physician and thrived in her role as a doctor for her community, but she still wished for more time to spend with her children—a normal and natural reaction for any working parent.

I'm in the same boat as so many Catholic mothers working forty hours a week outside the home and struggling to

---

[7]   Pietro Molla and Gianna Beretta Molla, *The Journey of Our Love: The Letters of Saint Gianna Beretta and Pietro Molla*, edited by Elio Guerriero (Pauline Books &Media, 2014).

balance faith, work, and family. In fact, there are over seven thousand of us in the Catholic Working Mothers Facebook group, all of us striving to follow God's will as wives, mothers, and employees. My experience with the group has taught me the importance of community. If you feel isolated and alone with no outlet to express your frustrations, the stress can pile up until it feels suffocating. Having the group as a pressure valve of sorts, as a source of sympathy and support, has helped me see that I'm not alone in my trials and troubles, which in turn has helped me bear them more patiently.

I wish the group had been around when I was a new working mother because I had so many questions about balancing my responsibilities to both God and my family with the responsibilities of my job.

I muddled through, doing the best I could, all the while thinking that I wasn't a "good enough" mom in the eyes of the Church because I couldn't stay at home with my kids. It took me a long time to realize that wasn't true, and an even longer time to form a community of Catholic working moms—a community that eventually led to my book, *The Catholic Working Mom's Guide to Life*.

The working mom life is still a difficult balancing act on the best of days, even with over fifteen years of work and six kids under my belt. Some days I feel like I'm barely keeping my head above water. But what really helps is knowing my priorities and keeping them in the right order—God, my spouse, my kids, and then my job.

As a member of the Catholic Working Mothers Facebook group said, "Your child needs to take precedence over your career. Always. Not saying that in a shaming way of 'you must stay home with your child.' Nope. Not that way at all. Continue to work! Enjoy your work! But remember, work is there to support the family. The family isn't there to support the work. The family unit is oh so important and has to be the focus at the end of the day. Your child will forever love you back, your job never will. Honor your child similarly."

You can do this, Mama. Keep your eyes on the cross because following Jesus will keep you on the right path.

JoAnna Wahlund

JoAnna Wahlund was baptized, raised, and married in the Evangelical Lutheran Church in America. In May 2003, two weeks after graduating from the University of Minnesota-Twin Cities with a degree in English, she converted to Catholicism. A North Dakota native, she fled the frigid north for the sunny skies of Arizona in 2008. She has six terrific kids here on earth, four saints in heaven praying for her, and a wonderful husband of seventeen years who supports her in all things. She worked outside the home as an editor for over a decade but now works as chief cook and bottle washer for La Casa Wahlund in addition to volunteering as Senior Editor for CatholicStand.com. Her website is www.catholicworkingmom.com.

Questions for Reflection

1. What circumstances and decisions are playing a part in your discernment to work during this season of motherhood? What has that discernment process looked like for you and your family?

2. Have you thought that you aren't good enough in the eyes of the Catholic Church if you're a working mom?

3. Who are women in your life who have encouraged you as a woman who is working and mothering? What are the ways they have come alongside you and accompanied you in this season?

Questions for Conversation

1. Does your job support your vocation (marriage) and the fruit of that vocation (your children)? What are some ways you can make sure you're keeping those priorities in the right order?
2. How has being a working mother challenged you? What are ways that you've felt encouraged by other women in this season?
3. What are some ways that family, friends, and our society can help support women who are working moms?

Come Holy Spirit, living in Mary. You know intimately the conflicts and joys that are the reality of my experience as a working mother. Help me to remember, especially on the more challenging days, that you work all things for good for those who love you. Equip me to show the light of your goodness to my family and coworkers as I become the woman you've made me to be. Amen.

$\mathcal{A}$ letter to the Woman with Children in Heaven

"Now I think I've cried a million tears for all the laughter we will never hear. We lost you in the silence before you had a chance to cry. You will always be my baby. You will always have my love. I will always, always be your mother. Always."
— J. J. Heller

I will always remember the first Mother's Day I celebrated as a mother. It didn't look like the holiday I'd been expecting. While I'd hoped that the day would be full of smiles and laughter as I celebrated with a little person growing steadily inside of me, instead I found myself dreading the holiday. Mother's Day will never be a holiday that I will celebrate in the way that I'd hoped and prayed for—with all of my children here with me on earth.

I never got to watch my body grow as our son, Marion, grew inside of me. My husband and I lost him to early miscarriage at just eight weeks. The experience of miscarriage was something I hadn't even thought to prepare for. But I quickly found out that one in four women experience a miscarriage. Despite being an awful event to have in common, the women I've met who have shared their story of motherhood and miscarriage have become my dear friends.

One woman whose friendship has been an incredible consolation in my life is Amy. I will forever be grateful for her witness to hope, joy, loss, and suffering. In a world that tells us that miscarriage is something that is normal and something to simply get over, Amy has taught me the beauty of honoring the lives of the children we will never get to meet this side of heaven.

If you're grieving the loss of a child who was gone before you had a chance to know him, sister, this letter is for you.

Dear sister,

One of the hardest parts about being a mother is learning to let our children go. They grow in our womb, we attend to their cries in the night, we rock them to sleep, we watch them take their first steps, we send them off to school, we hold our breath when they first start driving, and eventually we usher them out into the world. It can be such an unnatural feeling to let our children go.

But what about our children that we had to let go of before ever meeting them? I have ten saints in heaven and I've dreamed about each one of them. I've imagined their voices, wondered about their personalities, wished to hold them, and cried over the ache of not getting to know them. It's a brutally hard cross to bear.

I got pregnant with my oldest daughter when I was twenty-one. Her father and I were not married. It's safe to say we were not living out our Christian faith. However, Dustin and I loved each other heart and soul and we did marry two months after our daughter was born. Rhianna changed our lives in a thousand ways and all for the better. I will never forget the first time I looked at the little person who had been kicking me for the past several months. I had never seen anything so beautiful and perfect.

Our second daughter came along four years later. Our Sydney decided to come six weeks early and by emergency C-section. After I woke up from the anesthesia, they wheeled me up to the NICU to see her. I couldn't hold her, which is probably one of the surest forms of torture you can inflict on a mother—not allowing her to hold her baby. My arms ached to snuggle her, but all I could do was gently stroke her tiny arm as she lay in what seemed a plastic incubator. When I finally could hold her, it was like I could breathe again. At last I got to snuggle my tiny, precious sweet baby girl.

Life went on and a strange thing happened to me over time: I started to grow very selfish. When my husband would talk to me about having more kids, I would make every excuse in the book: I'd lose my figure, I wouldn't be able to work, it wasn't a good time, I'd have to pack a diaper bag again, etc.

While I had always envisioned having three children, I kept putting it off. Then I became pregnant, and shamefully, I was not happy about it. I hate to admit that but it's the truth. I was so blinded by my selfishness that I couldn't even be happy about the new life growing within me. Thankfully, though, it didn't take long for me to come around and begin to get excited about our new little one. Things started to look up . . . until the cramping started.

I vividly remember the ultrasound tech telling me that the baby had died. I just couldn't believe it. The doctor came in and very casually stated that "miscarriages were normal" and "yada, yada, yada." I wanted to punch him in the face. It was like it didn't even matter to him that my child was dead inside me.

I cried until I had no more tears to cry. That was the first of eight miscarriages that spanned nearly four years. Each one was utterly traumatic. I miscarried one baby while on the road traveling to my father-in-law's funeral. The guilt I felt over leaving my baby behind was horrific. I miscarried once while my husband was gone for work and I had to have a friend take me to the hospital. The eighth baby was miscarried not long after my husband left for deployment. My family did the best they could trying to support me, but it was agonizing being away from Dustin at such a time.

Because of so many miscarriages, I started to despair. No one would test me until the eighth miscarriage and, low and behold, we found out I had low levels of progesterone. My body did not make enough of the hormone to sustain a pregnancy. The doctor told us that if I ever did get pregnant again, as soon as I knew, I needed to get to the doctor as soon as possible for progesterone pills.

Once my husband came back from deployment, we talked about trying again. I was scared, but I was tired of being scared. I wanted to see the double lines on the pregnancy test and be happy, not fearful. So we decided to try again, but this time, we would both pray like never before. When I got pregnant, we embraced each other with smiles.

On May 4, 2014, we welcomed our Jeremiah. If I had given over to despair, I would never have known him. Somehow, God kept the flame of hope alive in me. Sadly, we have lost two babies after him even with getting on progesterone as soon as possible.

I think of my ten saints in heaven often. I've named them all: James, Lily, John, Ruth, Peter, Rebecca, Joseph, Elizabeth, Nicholas, and Rose. I don't know how many are really boys or girls, but I figure God can work out the details.

One of my greatest comforts is knowing that they have each other, and I feel great peace knowing that Our Mother Mary has them in her care. What I can say with certainty is that each one of these children has made me a better woman. They weeded out so much selfishness in my soul and helped me to see the true gift of children. I think I somewhat grasped this early on, but now I know it at my core.

I do believe something was truly medically wrong with me, and I don't believe that God caused my miscarriages in order to teach me a lesson. But through challenges and tragedies, God, in his fatherly way, always seeks to foster our continued growth. He sees it as an opportunity to mold us into better people if we allow him. He took this cross of mine and helped me to see the good that can come from it. I still struggle with selfishness, but not like I used to. I have learned to depend on God. I have ten saints that watch over me.

If you are a mother with littles in heaven, my heart goes out to you. It's darn hard to let them go. So many times, I begged for them to just stay with me, but it wasn't meant to be. For many in our society, having a miscarriage is just a "normal" thing, nothing to get that upset about.

This is nonsense. That baby is your baby no matter how small. A mother's love isn't based off the size of her child.

For most mothers with little ones in heaven, we carry them with us in the silence of our hearts. I have found that dealing with miscarriages runs you through the gamut of emotions. I've experienced guilt, anger, numbness, deep sadness, and fear. Today, I mostly feel a tender peace about it all. I still cry when I think about my little saints, but in a calmer way. I want you to know that it is okay to talk about them, miss them, dream about them, and love them. The world may say you shouldn't love a tiny being that you've never met, but the world doesn't get to decide that. The love of a mother is a beautiful thing, whether for her earthly children or her heavenly ones.

Rest assured, if we keep the faith, we will meet them someday. They will know us and we will know them and it will be glorious. Our tears will be gone and there will be nothing but love.

Be at peace, Momma. Your little ones in heaven are watching over you.

In Christ,

Amy Thomas

Amy Thomas converted to the Catholic faith in 2009. She is an Air Force military spouse, mother to three earthly children and ten heavenly ones. She's a homeschooling mom and a Catholic writer. Her weekly blogs can be found at www.catholicpilgrim.net. You can also connect with her on Facebook and Instagram. She recently released her new book, Reflections on the Book of James. When she isn't writing, she loves to travel, garden, listen to podcasts, study up on apologetics, cook, and read.

Questions for Reflection

1. What has your journey been like as a mother who has lost children to miscarriage?
2. Have you experienced fear, anxiety, or despair after losing a child to miscarriage? How does God desire to bring peace and hope to your story?
3. What are some ways that you can honor the life of the child you've lost to miscarriage? Have you named the child or children you've lost?

Questions for Conversation

1. How has your experiencing losing a child to miscarriage impacted your relationship with God, especially with God the Father?
2. What were some things that friends and family did to accompany you during your miscarriage(s) that were helpful? How did you see Christ in their actions?
3. How do you carry the child or children you've lost to miscarriage in your heart?

Come Holy Spirit, living in Mary. As I grieve the loss of my child to miscarriage, fill me with the hope that we have in Christ, the hope of the resurrection of the dead and life everlasting. Mary, wrap these children that we've lost here on earth in your mantle. Watch over them and journey with me as I strive towards heaven, where I hope to be reunited with them again.

A Letter to the Woman Whose Kids Are Crying at Mass

"Children cry, they are noisy, they don't stop moving. But it really irritates me when I see a child crying in church and someone says they must go out. God's voice is in a child's tears: they must never be kicked out of church."

—Pope Francis

The first Mass I went to with my newborn daughter went as smooth as it possibly could. She slept through the entire Mass, start to finish. But that experience was short lived. Quickly, Mass became an hour that I spent worrying about how much noise my daughter was making, what people were thinking of me as a parent, and how I was supposed to worship God and wrangle a squirming baby at the same time.

I know many women who have similar experiences—and maybe you have too, since you turned to this letter. I thought that what I needed was to return to that first Mass where my daughter was sleeping, not making a peep. But what I really needed was to rethink what I thought Mass was about.

When we go to Mass, we go to worship God. In this season of mothering young kids, loving them and teaching them about the beauty of the sacrament is an act of worshiping God too.

Katie is a woman whose words and wisdom have taught me so much about parenting. Her books have helped me introduce my daughter to the faith, and her friendship has been an encouragement during the weeks where taking kids to Mass seems more like a chore than an opportunity for worship.

If you're wondering if you'll ever be able to hear the words of consecration over the quiet whispers (or not-so-quiet tears) of your children, sister, this letter is for you.

Dear Sister,

For many years of my life, I went to Mass and had a prayerful, peaceful experience there. Now, it's different. The usher at my parish teases me as I walk into Mass, "I saved your spot!" pointing to a tile in the narthex where I find my escape mid-liturgy to calm my fidgeting one-year-old. It is different going to Mass with little ones. The trick, I've found, is to come to that place of gratitude for it being good-different.

But it doesn't come without a struggle. However, it is precisely in the struggle that I think we can learn so many things. When we miss the beauty amidst the chaos of attending Mass with little ones, we miss the glory of God at work in his most precious children and in us. Those seeds of faith and grace being planted every time we are at Mass are worth every toddler tear and mommy sigh. If we only knew the gift, I think we'd pay that price more often than just on Sundays.

Those hours truly reap eternal rewards, and those Masses can radically transform our perspective and our hearts.

Drawing near to his heart is right where Jesus wants our little ones—and us too. "Then children were brought to him that he might lay his hands on them and pray. The disciples rebuked the people; but Jesus said, 'Let the children come to me, and do not hinder them; for to such belongs the kingdom of heaven'" (Mt 19:13–14). The disciples tried to turn the mothers away, mothers who longed to have their little ones come even just a touch closer to the God of the Universe who created them. Do we have that longing as we approach Jesus with our children on Sunday?

Jesus could have said in response to his concerned disciples, "The children can come to my next gathering, but keep them quiet and in the back; they won't understand what's going on anyway." But he didn't. Jesus loved these children knowing their little developing selves would wiggle and giggle and whisper too loudly, need fairly constant reminders of how to be obedient and respectful, and require guidance as to what was being said and done. And today, still, he wants our children just as they are.

Our children can often teach us as much as we teach them (or more) at Mass. I love what Fr. Ryan Erlenbush has to say about this: "For me, as a priest, the sound of crying children calls to mind the mystery of the sacrifice of the Mass." He talks about how children's cries should remind us of the tears shed over the sacrifice at Calvary, as we often forget the greatness of Christ's offering for us. What a blessing to imagine that a child's cry should not merely inflict us with annoyance but instead remind us of the miracle happening right before our eyes and how our hearts should respond to it! This is just one example of the lessons we can learn simply by having our children present with us during the liturgy.

When it comes to feeling like our children, or we as their mothers, are unwelcome at Mass, sometimes it's our own insecurity we experience rather than real derision from onlookers. Though there are certainly those cantankerous parishioners who truly wish that all children, especially in church, would be seen and not heard, most of the people in Mass want the children to be there. They might be looking your way because they are just easily distracted, because they think your child is adorable, or because they actually believe your child is behaving better than you think they are! There have been times I've opened my mouth to apologize for my children as someone approached me after Mass and the other spoke first uttering compliments and not a single harsh word.

If our hearts are open to it, God will increase virtues in us: charity, patience, hope, diligence, and more. There are sometimes dozens of opportunities that present themselves throughout Mass urging us to opt for virtue growth over annoyance, frustration, or resignation. If we only look for and embrace these moments, we will find tremendous growth in our parenting and in our spiritual life. Going to Mass with little ones is truly a unique experience in this way.

Establishing rules is okay. Some of us have an inner voice of fear that informs us that if we are too rigid at church or have too many rules regarding our faith, our kids will be doomed to stray from the fold one day—all because of those rules of respect we had in place when they were two or three or seven. Goodness, let us not be so hard on ourselves. Guidelines and expectations are not drudgery; they are freeing. They help us, and our young ones, find the way to truly enjoy our experiences, especially the Mass. Adults follow patterns of behavior at Mass—we sit, stand, and kneel together. We are respectfully silent. We refrain from eating and distracting ourselves with gadgets. Having no expectations for your children at Mass may prevent them from learning how to fully engage in the miracle before them and in the love of a God who comes to meet them personally in the sacred liturgy. I recommend a spousal discussion, prayer, common sense, experience, and maybe even the Catholic blogosphere to help you figure out the right rules for your family. Perhaps surprisingly, your children may come to really appreciate those rules too.

After all, the Mass really isn't about us. It isn't about me having a prayerful experience. It isn't about my child behaving well. It isn't about the priest saying Mass without noisy interruption. It isn't about the church lady in the pew next to me having a perfectly peaceful liturgy. It's about worshipping God. Something we all can and should do. Our children's presence is their participation in worship. Sometimes our presence, in lieu of our prayers, is our worship. We may long to turn our hearts to him during the consecration in that prayerful, focused way we once knew, but instead find ourselves comforting a little knee bumped on the wooden pew. Let us give him that as worship, the unique offering of a mother at Mass.

Dearest mother and friend, I am in the trenches with you, but this is truly a trench I wouldn't have us escape too soon.

Every time we go to Mass, we can lament the challenge in front of us or we can embrace the opportunity to grow in virtue, while appreciating the reminders of life and hope that our children bring. As the common adage goes, "If you don't hear any crying, the church is dying."

Pope Benedict XVI once said, "To go to Mass together will be the light of Sunday for a family." In the little years, when our infants are crying and our toddlers are either trying to escape from the pew or making loud animal noises while crawling under the kneeler, Mass does not always— or maybe ever—feel like the light of this sacred day. Sometimes, we're just trying to make it through without too many eye rolls from others and too many trips to the potty.

But it won't always be that way. Someday, thanks to God's Eucharistic grace working in us and our resolution not to get discouraged or to give up on being present to Our Lord each Sunday in whatever state of life that finds us, maybe we will find that Mass really is the light of Sunday for our family. Or maybe in the midst of the chaos, we'll find that this is even true for us now. Either way, I imagine that when we come to this realization, which is accompanied by a deep sense of purpose for our family and the Catholic faith we hope will animate it, it will be us, and not our children, crying (happy tears) at Mass.

Blessings,

Katie

Katie Warner is a Catholic homeschooling mom and the author of several children's books including Father Ben Gets Ready for Mass *and*

This is the Church. *She is also the writer behind a popular prayer journal series including* A Parent Who Prays *and* A Spouse Who Prays. *Katie holds a graduate degree in Catholic Theology from the Augustine Institute, writes for the* National Catholic Register, *manages KatieWarner.com, and helps others home to the Church through Catholics Come Home. Katie lives in Georgia with her husband and fellow book-loving children.*

Questions for Reflection

1. How has worshipping at Mass with your children helped you grow in virtue as a mother?
2. What are some ways that you can help guide your child to participate in the liturgy of the Mass?
3. Is Mass on Sunday a light in the life of your family?

Questions for Conversation

1. How is worshipping God at Mass with your children different than worshipping at Mass before your children came? What differences are you grateful for?
2. What are ways you've struggled with bringing your children to Mass? Have you ever felt unwelcome at church because of your children?
3. What have you learned about the Mass and the liturgy from worshipping at Mass with your child? Has the way they've experienced and encountered Christ in the Eucharist changed the way that you worship Christ?

Come Holy Spirit, living in Mary. When my children make worshipping at Mass difficult or different, help me recognize that you are present here too. Help me to recognize you in the noise, tears, and squirms of my children. When I'm tempted to give into discouragement or despair, grow in me the virtues of charity, patience, hope, and diligence. Be with me as I bring these children to you, Lord. Amen.

A Letter to the Woman with Nothing to Wear

"Beauty is the arrowhead of evangelization."
—Bishop Robert Barron

How many times have you stared at your closet as you're getting ready and thought to yourself, "I have nothing to wear"? I know I've had that thought cross my mind many times. Before big events, I'm usually guilty of spending more time than I'd care to admit agonizing over what to wear and how I want to present myself. Maybe you, like me, have felt guilty for even thinking of clothes. Are our wardrobes something that we as Catholic women should put little thought into, writing fashion off as something frivolous?

Meghan's ability to speak into this struggle has been incredibly fruitful in my own life (and wardrobe!). She's taught me to recognize that the way we dress can reveal so much more than the latest trends and styles.

What if we could acknowledge the beauty that God has created in us and be drawn into a deeper relationship with him and awe of how good he is and the plans he has in store for us through how we dress?

If you're staring at your clothing and wondering where to even start, or you're feeling guilty for even worrying about your clothing, sister, this letter is for you.

Dear sister,

When it comes to style, you have to find your intention, you have to know your "why."

Why do you dress the way you do? Whom are you dressing for? What are you dressing for?

As Catholic women, we can be especially excited about fashion as Catholic women. Excuse me, come again? This could be a really strange statement because we might typically just think "I don't want to be vain" or "I don't want to be prideful" or "I should be spending my money on the poor." And yes, while these are true statements (and statements we should take seriously), just because they are true statements doesn't mean we can disregard other truths.

There are two other important (and easily forgotten) factors we should take into consideration: beauty and a contemplative spirit.

In the *City of God*, St. Augustine points out that "beauty is indeed a good gift of God." Beauty is an aspect of God. And since it's an aspect of God, we should likewise create a disposition in our hearts to cultivate a sense of beauty. Simply put, we ought to do things beautifully.

And secondly, while we're doing things beautifully, we should also do things with a contemplative spirit. In St. Therese's words, "Do all things with love." So just as we clean the bathroom with love, cook for our families with love, or wrap a gift with love, we can also get dressed with love. Yes! We can do a simple thing like getting dressed in the morning for God.

I'm super blessed to really live out the feminine genius as a fashion consultant. As a woman, I think one of our best qualities is to nurture and encourage. And I think as women, we can take two routes. We can either tear each other down or we can be a source of encouragement.

The effects of nurturing and encouraging a woman, with guided helpful steps and knowledge, have remarkable outcomes that have the power to make me well up with tears! Many times when I work with my clients, I see an inner transformation happen. When a woman acknowledges the beauty and dignity God gave her, it shines through, and using clothes is a way to realize this and express it. I often hear and see the beauty that blossoms in a woman's soul when she takes the time to highlight her unique beauty.

And the vehicle to get this outcome is clothing! While I'm obviously not a philosopher, I know what I see and experience. In my experience, when a woman invests in her style and dresses with respect, her attitude and other aspects of her life positively change.

More than half of American women feel frustrated with their clothing and feel like they don't have anything that feels flatters their body *and* personality. So you are not alone if you feel this way. The good news is that there are simple steps you can take today if you want to change the way you view clothes and the way you dress.

If you're thinking of diving into your "style journey" (I mean, what do you have to lose?), the first thing I want to tell you is not to be discouraged. It's easy to get overwhelmed and think you don't have the right amount of money, the "perfect" body, or "the eye" for aesthetics.

But let me tell you, none of that matters. Really! With whatever shape, budget, or aesthetic you have, you *can* enjoy your wardrobe and you *can* find your style!

With that said, a big part of not getting discouraged is not comparing yourself to your peers. Sure, you can find inspiration from them, and this is even recommended! However, if you find yourself about to make a comparison, stop for a moment and comment on their style positively, while not belittling yourself. Let yourself appreciate their unique beauty while also respecting your own.

Once you've got this covered, you just have to be very practical with your plan to discover your style.

The first step to define your personal style is to make a list of style icons. They can be typical, like Princess Kate or Grace Kelly, and they can be unique, like a specific character you admire from a movie or TV show.

Secondly, you'll want to develop a personal mood board (Pinterest is a perfect tool for this). Just as with anything else you do, when you write it down, map it out, and make a plan, your ideas will more likely become a reality. Since fashion is visual, it's best to be tangible with styles we take delight in and which silhouettes highlight our beauty.

Once you've been developing your eye towards the style you want to emulate, you need to make a shopping list. This should be a prioritized list of key, versatile items that will expand your options with clothes you already have. Most often, these will be key foundational pieces like a classic black dress, a white oxford button-down, a winning jean, or a flattering wrap dress that you can easily dress up or down with the appropriate shoes, layers, and accessories. Yep, just like you go to the grocery store with a food list, you need to have a wardrobe list. I mean, can you imagine going to the grocery store without a shopping list? The rare times I've done this, I've come out with things I do not need and that only pleased my palette in that moment. We don't want to do this with our closets. The key is to be super intentional and follow the roadmap you've laid out for your style.

These really are simple, easy steps to transform your wardrobe and begin to enjoy your style. With time, a prayerful spirit, a positive attitude, and a little bit of fun, focusing on your style will soon change the woman you are.

Of course, it's not that clothes magically change you. Rather, you are changed by living intentionally through doing the "little things" with love and expressing that "beauty is indeed a good gift from God!"

Meghan

For the past seven years, Meghan has worked in Los Angeles and San Francisco as a Fashion Stylist. Most recently before working specifically with Catholic women, she was the Head Stylist of Allume, a burgeoning Silicon Valley Personal Styling Start-Up. She now lives between the South of France and Austin, TX with her husband! To learn more about her styling business, you can subscribe to her Friday emails on her website at www.meghanashleystyling.com. You can also follow along with her travels and style tips on Instagram at @meghanashleystyling. If you're interested in working with Meghan (or have a style question!), simply email her at meghan.ashley.styling@gmail.com.

Questions for Reflection

1. What do the clothes you own reveal about who you are? Do they accurately represent your personality and the woman God has created you to be?

2. How can you encounter the clothes hanging up in your closet and folded in your drawers with a contemplative spirit? What would that look like in your daily life as a Catholic woman?

3. Are there any changes that you need to make to your wardrobe so that it highlights your unique beauty as a daughter of God?

Questions for Conversation

1. As a Catholic woman, have you felt ashamed for taking an interest in clothing, or being passionate about finding beauty in what you wear? How can clothing be something that glorifies God and who he has made you to be?

2. Do you feel frustrated with your clothing? What are some clothing choices you've worn that have flattered both your body and your personality?

3. Who are some style icons who inspire the way you dress and what you look for when it comes to putting together an outfit?

Come Holy Spirit, living in Mary. You've created a world filled with beauty and you invite me to contemplate it. Help me to encounter this beauty in the little things—like the way that I get dressed for the day and the clothing that I put in my closet. When I'm tempted to compare my closet or figure to the women around me, help me recognize their belovedness as your daughters and rejoice that I'm your beloved daughter too. Amen.

A Letter to the Woman Getting Out of Her Comfort Zone

"I will seize the occasions that present themselves every day; I will accomplish ordinary actions in an extraordinary way"
—Cardinal François-Xavier Nguyên van Thuân

I'm very familiar with my own comfort zones. Too familiar, in fact. It's difficult for me to rouse myself out of this cozy comfort and grow in trusting God and his plan for me. So when my sister, Madysen, started pushing outside her own comfort zone and expressing a desire to live a great life for God, I knew I needed to pay attention.

Madysen has encouraged me to push out of my comfort zone and strive for holiness in my everyday life. Her magnanimity and courage inspire me to strive for greatness and the Lord in my own life as a Catholic woman.

She's lived a life of adventure, but the adventure that I'm the most proud to witness is the adventurous life she's living for Christ and because of her relationship with him. It's the insights from her time in prayer, her radical trust, and her courage in conversation that inspire me more so than her ability to hike to any height or travel to any location without fear.

If you're desiring a life of greatness for the Lord but know that he will have to stretch your heart to his will and his plans for you, sister, this letter is for you.

Dear sister,

When I was eighteen, I was offered a chance to go to Nicaragua for two weeks with my university. I knew no Spanish at all and vaguely knew two of the other two girls who went. Before this trip, I'd never been away from my family for more than a night. This was a textbook case for stepping out of my comfort zone.

I remember walking outside the airport in Managua and breathing in the warm air, looking up at the night sky, and wondering how I could go back to regular life after this. It was a crazy two weeks. I swam in an imploded volcano lake. I lived with a host family who spoke no English. I learned to be okay not wearing makeup or caring about my appearance. I pushed my comfort zone in so many ways.

Pope Benedict XVI has a quote in his encyclical letter *Spe Salvi* that states, "Man was created for greatness—for God himself; he was created to be filled by God. But his heart is too small for the greatness to which it is destined. It must be stretched."

As an eighteen-year-old fresh out of a small town and with a homeschooled K–12 background, I wanted greatness. I wanted to try everything and see everywhere and have crazy stories to tell when I came back home for a visit. But that's not what this quote is about. That's not what greatness is.

Pushing your comfort zone by chopping all your hair off can be good. Stretching your comfort level by planning a last minute trip to Indonesia can also be good. But comfort zones aren't confined to huge crazy decisions. Something like trying a new flavor of latte is stepping out of your comfort zone. Reading a science fiction book when it's not really your genre is growth. I didn't figure it out until junior year of college, but pushing my comfort zone spiritually was the biggest adventure I've ever had—more so than backpacking across Spain for a month (I still didn't know any Spanish) or moving across the country to a city where I didn't know anyone.

Spiritually, I was about as adventurous as a sloth. I grew up Catholic, went to Mass every Sunday, listened to Bible stories that my mom read, and prayed the Rosary daily. But I wasn't in a relationship with God. He was just sort of there. My faith was super comfortable. Living my faith didn't push any limits for me.

I was a cozy Catholic. Why? I had never had to accept my faith or own it or stand up for it. It was a hand-me-down sweater from my parents and I wore it faithfully, but I didn't understand why I had it on. But when I got to college, my faith was challenged by a classmate. He made a comment about the sexual abuse scandal during class, and I had to decide if I wanted to stand up and out myself as Catholic to defend this religion that I wasn't really sure I understood or if I was just going to stay on my comfortable couch of a religion and ignore him. Spoiler alert: I pushed my comfort zone. But it wasn't easy! It was super uncomfortable and I probably ended up confusing both of us. But the more that I researched why I believed what I did, the more I understood and the more I fell in love with God.

So what does it mean to me to push comfort zones? A close friend once told me, "Do not ask if it will be hard. Ask rather if it will be good." Is it hard to learn about why the Church teaches x, y, and z and still stand with her? Yes. Is it good? Yes. Is it hard to go for a three-day backpacking trip through the Grand Canyon? Yes. Is it good? Yes. Is it hard to branch out and choose a different flavor of ice cream? Not really, but it's good!

Comfort zones are familiar. But when God made you, he imagined a strong, brave, beautiful woman who will become a saint. We have to put in the effort to become great. We can stretch our hearts in small ways, continually widening them so that we become magnanimous. I hope you (and I!) don't let fear stand in the way of becoming the woman God created you to be. Push your comfort zone today—big or small, it will be good.

In Jesus through Mary,

Madysen

Madysen Mooradian is a Kansas native who now resides in the Phoenix area. She has a degree in Anthropology and is still working on finding a "grown up" job, but right now she works as a barista as she trusts in his timing. Madysen spends most of her free time outdoors: hiking, kayaking, and running, but when she's not doing those things, she's cooking or country swing dancing. Madysen is convinced that if Blessed Pier Giorgio Frassati were alive today, they would be best friends.

Questions for Reflection

1. What are small (and large!) ways that you can strive for greatness and magnanimity in your life today?
2. Where is the Lord inviting you to step out of your comfort zone in your spiritual life and your relationship with him?
3. Has there been something that is hard (but good!) that you've accomplished with the help of God? What did that experience teach you?

Questions for Conversation

1. What has been a time in your life when God has pushed you outside your comfort zone? How did your respond?
2. Have you ever had to defend your faith to someone? Did the experience help you grow in knowledge and love of God?
3. Who is a woman in your life who has inspired you with the way she strives for greatness and holiness in her daily life?

Come Holy Spirit, living in Mary. You've created me for greatness, but my heart is too small to accept this magnanimous mission in my daily life. Stretch my heart, my comfort zones, and the limits that I have put on myself and you, Lord. Inspire me to live a life totally devoted to you and your will for me, your daughter. Amen.

A Letter to the Woman Sitting in Adoration

*"Heaven for me is hidden in a little host where
Jesus, my spouse, is veiled for love. I go to that
Divine Furnace to draw out life, and there my
Sweet Savior listens to me night and day."*
—St. Therese of Lisieux

I grew up going to adoration hours with my parents and siblings. I have many fond memories of growing up sitting in the pews of our local adoration chapel, my mom explaining what it meant to sit and adore Christ. But it wasn't until I was getting ready to start college that I realized what it meant to be loved by God and to desire to grow in relationship with him in the Eucharist.

But even after countless adoration hours and beautiful experiences with Christ in the Blessed Sacrament throughout the years, sometimes I'm still left wondering how to pass an hour with him in the little adoration chapel close to my house.

Sara has taught me about both simply existing with the Lord and actively responding to his will in our lives as Catholic women. She has a radical trust in Christ and his plan for her life.

If you've ever sat in adoration and wondered how to grow in relationship with Christ in the Eucharist, sister, this letter is for you.

Dear sister,

Dusk was descending on a regular Tuesday evening. I had pressing thoughts and pending decisions swirling around my mind. So I hopped in my car, drove to a church where I knew the doors would be unlocked this late in the day, and took my burdens to Jesus.

When I arrived, I was shocked at the number of cars in the parking lot on an average weekday night. I tentatively stepped through the front door, into the narthex, and peeked into the sanctuary to find out what was going on.

To my surprise, the monstrance was on the altar, the candles were lit, and incense was rising in the air—Eucharistic adoration! My heart began to sing. I came to Jesus and he came to me. Eyes locked on him, I slowly made my way to a pew near the front, singing along "O Salutaris Hostia" with the small group of people gathered there.

As I slipped into the pew and dropped to my knees, I caught sight of the flowers placed on the altar. Out of the middle of the bouquet sprang a beautiful gladiolus—one of the flowers I had insisted on having on the altar on my wedding day. Seeing those flowers drove home a message, loud and clear.

Jesus was here for me. Jesus poured out his love for me, his beautiful bride.

With peace in my heart and tears in my eyes, I began my hour with him. What did I do for an entire hour in a still, quiet church? What do you do when you spend an hour with those you love the most?

When I spend an hour with my best friend, we chat about anything and everything. I share the deepest parts of my heart and ask for her advice. We reminisce about old stories and dream about the future. An hour with my best friend passes in the blink of an eye.

When I spend an hour with my dad, we sit in silence and enjoy each other's company. We don't need a lot of words to communicate the love between us. Sometimes we look out at the world together. Sometimes we work side by side, quietly sharing a task. An hour with my dad is a time of peace, strength, and grounding.

When I spend an hour with my toddler, I snuggle close and hold him tight. I read him books and sing him songs. I pour out my love for him, and he loves me in return. At times, we find so much peace together that we drift off to sleep.

When I spend an hour with my husband, we laugh and tease, we discuss and debate. We rejoice about the life we've built together and plan for what's to come. We share our desires, our fears, and our random thoughts. An hour with my husband makes me feel known and treasured.

When you spend an hour with Jesus, you are face-to-face with the one who loves you with an infinite love. The best thing to do is to spend this time with Our Lord as you would spend time with your best friend, a beloved parent, a child, or a spouse.

You can chat with him about anything and everything, as you would a friend. Pour out the deepest parts of your heart to him and ask for his advice. Tell him what's going on in your life right now and what your dreams for the future are. You may find that an hour chatting with Jesus as your best friend passes in the blink of an eye.

You can sit quietly with him and enjoy each other's company. You may not need a lot of words. Perhaps you can gaze out at the world with him, taking in your life as a whole. Or you can work together through a particular task or topic of discernment, side-by-side with Jesus to lean on. An hour with Jesus can be a time of peace, strength, and grounding.

You can pass the time drawing close to Jesus and holding him tight, clinging to him with love and affection. You may read spiritual books or sing songs of praise in your heart. You can pour out your love for him and allow him to love you in return. You might find that you drift off to sleep during Adoration, overcome by the peace of his presence.

You can spend an hour with Our Lord in intense and dynamic love, as you would with a spouse. You may find yourself overcome with joy or sharing the deepest grief. You can rejoice with him over the blessings he has given you, or wrestle with your interior conflicts and crosses. Share your desires, your fears, and even your random thoughts with him. Communing with Jesus so intimately can let you feel known and treasured by him.

However you choose to spend your time with Jesus is beloved and pleasing to him. Whatever your time in Adoration looks like, don't try to force it. Simply place yourself in his presence and let him do the rest.

Seek him, and he will come to you, lead you, guide you, and inspire you. Know that he is waiting to love you with his perfect love. Open your heart to receive his love and love him in return.

Jesus is here for you.

Jesus pours out his love for you, his beautiful bride. Don't worry about what you are going to do or say. Just give him your heart, and that is enough.

Sara

Sara Estabrooks is a Catholic wife, mom, and author who loves the mystery of the Holy Eucharist. On her blog To Jesus, Sincerely, *Sara loves to chat about the universal call to holiness, practical application of the virtues, and building a better prayer life. When your days are crazy, visit her website, Facebook, or Instagram pages if you need a place where you can find encouragement to keep on seeking a stronger relationship with Christ. If you are looking for inspiration about parenting, tune in to the podcast* Home But Not Alone, *where Sara and her co-host Tim Lucchesi have uplifting conversations about real life as a Catholic stay-at-home parent. Sara is also the author of* Becoming Holy, One Virtue at a Time, *from Our Sunday Visitor, a book that will guide you in living out the theological and cardinal virtues.*

Questions for Reflection

1. What has been your experience praying with the Lord during Eucharistic adoration?
2. Do you find it easy to place yourself in Christ's presence while you pray in adoration? What has kept you from simply abiding in the Lord's presence?

3. How can you open yourself up to receive the love and presence of Christ in your everyday life?

Questions for Conversation

1. What are some ways that you've spent time in adoration with Christ in the Eucharist?
2. Is there a chapel for Eucharistic adoration near where you live? Have you considered having a dedicated hour in your week for spending time with the Lord? If there's not an opportunity for adoration, what are other ways you can adore the Lord in the Eucharist?
3. How would you spend an hour with the person you love the most? What does reflecting on this question reveal to you about ways you can spend time in adoration with Christ in the Eucharist?

Come Holy Spirit, living in Mary. As I encounter the beauty and reality of Christ present in the Eucharist, help me to simply abide in this moment. Free me from distractions and help me to find rest. Give me the grace of receptivity so that I can open my heart to the complete and total love of Christ and adore him in the Eucharist. Amen.

Conclusion

*"Each woman who lives in the light of eternity can
fulfill her vocation, no matter if it is in marriage,
in a religious order, or in a worldly profession."*
—St. Teresa Benedicta of the Cross

As women today, the *last* thing we need is another thing to add to our already too long to-do lists. Because if your to-do list is anything like mine, we're not getting to the bottom of it anytime soon, and that can be exhausting. But living out the feminine genius in our daily lives isn't about what we *do* as women. Instead, it's about who we *are* as women.

Each woman's feminine genius is unique and essential to society and to the Church. No matter what your vocation, your season of life, your talents, your joys, or your struggles, the feminine genius is for you. Every one of the women who shared a letter in this book lives out the feminine genius uniquely in her own everyday life. None of them embrace the feminine genius in the exact same way, even though some of them may be living in the same season of life or pursuing God's will in the same vocation.

Some of the women who wrote letters shared about how they live out the feminine genius in their vocation of marriage, like Emily Ricci's vocation with her husband, Aaron, or Amanda Teixeira's marriage that she spoke about in her letter. This feminine genius is also at work in the lives of women who are single, discerning where the Lord is calling them—which Sarah Burns and Nicole Guarascio live out beautifully in their daily lives.

The feminine genius can be embraced in seasons of motherhood, and that maternity is unique for each woman too. Maybe you're called to adoptive motherhood, like Mary Bruno. Perhaps you're the mother to children you haven't gotten to hold this side of heaven, like Amy Thomas. Or maybe you're in a season of discerning how best to live out your feminine genius with your family, like Emily Frase and JoAnna Wahlund talked about in their letters. Our maternity as women living out the feminine genius can also manifest itself through spiritual maternity in relationship with others, like the way that Julia Marie Hogan journeys with women to grow in healthy self-care practices, or the way that Beth Williby encourages women to reject the lies of comparison in their daily lives.

But regardless of each woman's vocation and season of life, each woman possesses the feminine genius. It's inherent to who we are as women. God has created us with the feminine genius already in place in our very soul. It's not something we have to earn or something we have to do. Instead, it's someone we are, the women we're becoming as we discover God's will in our lives.

Words can't describe how excited I am for you to continue to discover and embrace this feminine genius in your life. I can't wait to see how you live out the feminine genius in your unique and beautiful way that only you can do. I know without a doubt that God has amazing plans in store for you and your feminine genius, sister.

In his Sacred Heart,